THE POETRY WRITING HANDBOOK

NEIL BALDWIN

SCHOLASTIC BOOK SERVICES
New York Toronto London Auckland Sydney Tokyo

ISBN 0-590-31718-0

12 11 10 9 8 7 6 5 4 3 2 1   9   1 2 3 4 5 6/8

Printed in the U. S. A.   06

For reprint permission grateful acknowledgement is made to:

Alfred A. Knopf, Inc. for "Autobiographia Literaria" from *Selected Poems of Frank O'Hara* by Frank O'Hara, copyright © 1967 by Maureen Granville-Smith, Administratrix of the Estate of Frank O'Hara.
The Asia Society for "The Ideal Retreat" translated by W.S. Merwin with Nguyen Ngoc Bich, from *Selected Translations 1948-1968* (Atheneum, New York) by W.S. Merwin, copyright © 1967 by W.S. Merwin.
Robert Bly for "Snowfall in the Afternoon" from *Silence in the Snowy Fields*, published by Wesleyan University Press, 1962, copyright © 1962 by Robert Bly.
Harper & Row, Publishers, Inc. for "One Home" from *Stories That Could Be True* by William Stafford, copyright © 1960 by William Stafford.

Poems

you write a poem
wondering
will it be good or bad
does it rhyme
or is it like a story
hoping your publisher
will like it
if not
you may have to start all over again

Renee, grade 5

Read the poems you like reading. Don't bother whether they're "important" or if they'll live. What does it matter what poetry *is*, after all? If you want a definition of poetry, say, "Poetry is what makes me laugh or cry or yawn, what makes my toenails twinkle, what makes me want to do this or that or nothing," and let it go at that. All that matters about poetry is the enjoyment of it, however tragic it may be.

—Dylan Thomas, "Poetic Manifesto" (1951)

Acknowledgments

Ten years have passed since I first became seriously involved with poetry and teaching. Many people have helped me arrive at the point where I was able to write this book.

Joanne Allison, when she was Director of the Kenan Center in Lockport, New York, gave me the opportunity to teach my first poetry workshop for children.

Myra Klahr, Executive Director of New York State Poets-in-the-Schools, welcomed me into the program and provided me with an open forum so that, as a young poet, I could try out my developing theories in the classroom.

Several other friends, fellow poets, and administrators have given me inspiration, encouragement, and guidance in a difficult field: Robert Creeley, Barbara Danish, Audrey Feuerstein, June Fortess, Esther Harriot, Richard Huttner, David Ignatow, John Logan, Roberta Plutzik, Steven Schrader, Nancy Larson Shapiro, and Galen Williams.

Thanks to all the poets — whose poems form the basis for these lessons — for responding so generously to my requests for further comments about the genesis of their work.

And thanks to all the district superintendents and principals in Western New York who allowed me into their schools; to all the teachers who invited me into their classrooms; and to all the children who wrote so beautifully: Their poems make this book what it is.

N.B.
Brooklyn Heights, NY
Spring, 1981

CONTENTS

INTRODUCTION

◆

*The Importance
of Poetry
in the Classroom*

◆

This is an activity book for English and language arts teachers in grades four through nine; a handbook of fifteen interrelated lesson plans on poetry writing.

This book will show you how to introduce children to the pleasures of poetry and how to create an environment in which poetry writing can occur. It will be your guide through an exploration with your students into the nature of poetry. The results will be poems of honesty and simplicity. The poems upon which the lessons are based are classroom-tested. Quite simply, they *work* as stimuli to get children writing.

Over a three-year period, as a member of the Poets-in-the-Schools program in upstate New York, I conducted poetry workshop series—using the very same poems as are included here—in more than 50 elementary and secondary schools. I worked with more than 150 teachers and 4,000 children. My classes were not "special" or "gifted," and the children were not pulled out or selected from their peer groups as being unusually talented in writing. The schools were in urban, suburban, and rural areas, as you will be able to tell from the subject matter of the children's poems that follow.

No special credentials are needed to pursue this course of teaching and learning. All you have to do is be willing to read and consider what may at first seem to be new and different types of writing; accept the appropriateness of expressing feelings in the classroom; and accept the vocabulary and language of children as suitable for a poem.

s not have to be taught in a way that
te departure from the manner in which
jects are taught. Poetry writing is, indeed,
a but it is a creative task. It is difficult, but
it is also enjoyable.

Learning about poetry differs from other kinds
of more formal expository and narrative writing.
There must be a conscious balance of structure with
freedom. We must be made to feel free to give voice
to our deepest feelings. However, the terms "free
verse" and "blank verse" are misleading, implying
that all you have to do is get your thoughts down
on paper in streams of consciousness, contrive a
rhyme scheme, and presto! the poem's done. It's
not that simple.

The Lessons

Each lesson in this book centers upon some basic
poetic *concept* (i.e., "form" or "image") or poetic
theme (i.e., "memory," "self-portrait," or "environment"). Each lesson incorporates all of the following steps (which are elaborated upon in more
detail in the next chapter):

1. *Reading aloud* a poem by an American poet;
and *listening* to the poem being read, several times,
by different members of the class, including the
teacher.

2. Brief *discussion* and *questions* about some of the
general ideas and themes in the poem.

3. Emphasis upon the poetic *concept* or *theme*
central to the day's particular lesson, with extensive
use of the blackboard.

4. *Reading aloud* of student-written poems in the book as examples of what is possible.

5. *Writing* in class based upon the discussion, questions, and readings, with focus upon the concept or theme of the day.

6. *Reading aloud* what has been written.

Every class session includes basic interrelated skills of reading, listening, and writing. Not only are these important skills emphasized and reemphasized, but also the way in which they fit together and work together as *poetry*.

The lesson plans are arranged cumulatively. Skills and concepts acquired in earlier phases are referred to and applied later on. Of course, you as the classroom teacher know your own students best of all, and you have the option of picking the book up at any point and making use of it as you see fit.

Reading aloud and discussion usually take the first half of a forty-five-minute class session, and writing, the second. We're not interested in making literary critics out of ten-year-olds! Our intention is to set an atmosphere, create a mood. The advantage of this approach is that each lesson is completely structured to lead eventually to tangible results, written or spoken.

The Poems

The poems I've chosen for the lessons are the poems of today, based upon everyday life, written in direct and simple language. They contain no stilted diction; only occasional end rhyme (although there certainly are echoes and repeating vowel sounds that you will hear when you read them aloud); no "iambic pentameter" as such (although there certainly is a rhythm to the words and phrases).

These poems are extensions of the way we talk. Their language is not abstract or separated from life. They were written by real people who lived (or now live) in the world, and who have translated their experiences into poetic, common language.

Such a view of poetry helps make the writing of it useful to children. The only theme (with variations, as we shall see) is themselves. Perhaps, by making a record of some of their experiences, they'll come to view themselves and what they do in more positive ways. Your classroom will become personalized. As the children hear the poems of their peers and friends and share what's been written, they will be brought closer together as people.

Their poems will not, however, plug in to prescribed forms (sonnet, haiku, cinquaine, etc.). The form their poems take will come out of the children's feelings and moods at the time of writing. You will be able to show them how to "set up" the poems properly, but there will not be any bending of thoughts to fit a mold.

You will notice a narrative thread in most of the example poems here, a logical sequence of events or images following upon each other, as the poet attempts to make order out of the confusion of life. Likewise, you'll move through the discussion of the poem with a carefully ordered series of questions about what is happening in the poem; what the children feel as they hear it, read it, and think about it.

Poetry in Everyday Life

A writer tries to do a little of his craft every day, whether it be a letter, a brief postcard, or a few notes and jottings, just to keep the wheels turning. And as the days go by, the little bits and pieces add up until something *whole* comes of them. The same principle applies to the classroom. The children begin to see that they are building toward writing. They will *want* to see results. Even if each and every lesson does not conclude with a polished poem, sooner or later they will come.

Just as a piano player does not practice an entire piece of music every day, the writer keeps his mind moving with some kind of writing. Many of your students undoubtedly play musical instruments, or enjoy one sport above all others. They understand that if you want to be a better piano player or base-ball player, you've got to *do* it. The more the better.

It all begins with the poem as narrative. Who does not remember the joy of being read to? The children are put at ease; their only responsibility at the beginning is to concentrate upon the words. Then they will begin to read poems as *writers* of poetry, with an enhanced awareness of what the poem they read has to teach them about their *own* future poems.

The primary concern of this new, poem-centered curriculum is the relationship of the young student to his world—of other people, and of experiences. We will go a long way toward solving the perennial problem of "what to write about" once we broaden the territory of poetry.

This book helps you introduce the subject matter of everyday life as the true subject matter for poetry.

How to Use
This Book

The Poem
Biographical note about the poet
Commentary

---

1. Introduction
2. Teacher reads poem aloud
3. Children read poem aloud
4. Questions
5. The concept and/or theme
6. What we will write about
7. Children's poems from the book
8. Reread poem, restate task
9. Writing
10. Read aloud what is written

The Poem. You will find it helpful to spend some time alone with the poem the night before you will be introducing it in class. Think about it, read it through several times, to achieve familiarity with it in your own way.

Biographical note about the poet. This section may include brief remarks by the poet detailing the situation in which the poem was written. We do not want to overload the children with too much background information before they have had the chance to come to their own conclusions.

Commentary. I've included some of my own thoughts about the poem to provide a context, and help guide you through it. I will point out "signposts" within the poem as an aid toward increased awareness.

---

1. **Introduction.** You are in class. The children wait expectantly. The first thing you do is write any difficult words from the poem—which will be indicated as such—and the central theme and/or key concept for the day, on the blackboard. When introducing the poem, make use of any conclusions you've come to in reading it on your own the previous night, any biographical information you'd like to provide, and any aspect of my commentary you think will help.

2. **Teacher reads poem aloud.** Move right into the poem with a minimum of fanfare. You might

ask the children to close their eyes, and wait until there is no sound in the room. The more relaxed and concentrated on your voice they are the better. This will also help the children remember, as they will not have the poem in front of them. Unless otherwise indicated, the only copy of the poem available will be the one in this book. Read slowly and clearly. Don't worry about observing line breaks. The pauses will occur naturally once you have achieved familiarity with the poem. After you have finished reading, don't say anything for a few moments; try to sustain the silence—not reverentially, but just to let the words sink in.

3. Children read poem aloud. Levels of embarrassment vary from class to class. Always ask for a volunteer first; someone will take the plunge, especially after you have demonstrated your fearlessness! Hand him or her your copy of the book. Wherever possible, as you can see, we have tried to fit the poem into one page, or two facing pages, so it can be seen in its entirety. Let two or three children read the poem. Listen for inevitable variations of inflection and cadence, changing the poem from person to person. Bring this fact to their attention as it happens. All we are doing up to this point is reading and listening—*not* interpreting.

4. Questions. A series of questions is provided, based upon the poem, falling into two broad categories. *First*, we want to arrive at a sense of the poem as an emotional experience. The questions are designed to start the children wondering, conjecturing, projecting themselves into the mind of the speaker and into the way the poem makes them feel when they hear it. What mood does it put them in? We are still less concerned with what the poem means than with the atmosphere it creates.

Second, we focus upon the details and facts in the poem as far as can be determined. Who is speaking? Where is he or she? What is happening? How do we know? How would you explain this poem to someone else? Let's say it was written in a language that you alone could understand, and you wanted to explain it to your friend. How would you translate it into English? A question like "What is happening in this poem?" is far preferable to "What does the poet mean by . . . ?"

Seek a diversity of answers. When someone does answer, nod your head, indicate acceptance, and move on. "Does everyone agree with what . . . just said?" Let the class see that different points of view are possible. The emphasis is on *perception*, not interpretation. Rather than trying to second-guess the poet (which is impossible), we should seek out what it is in the poem that speaks to us, enjoying it for what it *is*.

5. The poetic concept and/or theme. Some classes will be focused upon what might also be called "mechanics" or poetics in addition to a subject for writing. The book is set up so that important themes *build* toward a basic awareness of poetry. We begin with a discussion of *form*. How do poems look? How are they set up? We also learn about the *line* as a basic unit of a poem, leading to *rhyme*.

11

Defining *image* (pictures from words) leads naturally to *imagination*. Self-portraits and variations on that rich theme allow the children to make up word pictures of themselves and others. Each child finds his or her own *voice*, his personal way of saying things.

Finally, we concentrate upon poems about the world around us, people and places we know or have known well. We come to terms with how a poem looks and how it is presented; then we learn how to make our *word pictures* as sharp and clear as we can.

6. What we will write about. The assignment coming at the conclusion of the discussion must be stated clearly. If the assignment is well-framed, writing will happen.

If you tell the children *too much*, you destroy that all-important spontaneity. If you tell them *too little*, they'll be stranded in unfamiliar territory. There has to be room for improvisation, which, in turn, becomes limited by a growing awareness of what is right for each poem.

I've tried to describe the subject as clearly as possible. I hope you will refine the script when necessary.

7. Children's poems from the book. This is an optional step. "Here are some poems on this same subject, written by children in other schools . . . ." It may help your class to hear the work, so they can understand what is possible, what has been done by others, and therefore can certainly be done by them. Leave this out if you think your students will be intimidated.

8. Reread poem, restate task. Lead into writing by reading the poem to the children one more time, and by making certain that all students understand what they are to write about. I have also included "spin-off" subjects for those children who are ready and able to improvise. You can tell whether it's safe to provide options, or whether this will be confusing.

9. Writing. You should now have about twenty minutes of your forty- or forty-five-minute class period remaining. This will be enough time for the children to do a first draft. I have found that much more time than this can lead to daydreaming or more distracting pursuits that interfere with the mood. Try to group the children at tables of no more than six or eight. While they are writing, you can circulate and help them with additional problems. Children sitting next to each other can exchange papers. This would also be the time when you choose to jot down some lines of your own making.

10. Read aloud what is written. Save a few minutes just before the end for a brief reading session: "All right, who wants to read his/her poem to the rest of us?" Expect silence at first. Offer to read it for someone. Ask the authors if they'd be willing to have someone else in class read their work. If you have managed to write something, try making a deal with some venturesome child: you'll read yours if she'll read hers. Obviously, this should not be made into anything resembling a compulsory activity. Again, as time passes, students will come forward. The first few minutes of the next class meeting can be used to read poems from the previous class. You might also set up a formal poetry reading at the end of the year, or take your students into another class and make a presentation to them. These options are discussed elsewhere in the book.

A word about format. The lessons are written in the first person, as if they were "scripts" for classroom use. For the sake of clarity, I've therefore eliminated quotation marks. My own comments are set off by parentheses and indented from the main flow of the lesson.

We are ready to begin. The lessons that follow are very structured; but remember not to expect predetermined structure in the children's poems. You will set a scene, provide the incentive, enable the children to write. Their poems will take shapes as various as their imaginations!

THE LESSONS

◆

Part I
Searching
Within

◆

Earliest memory

My Grandmother's Love Letters

There are no stars to-night
But those of memory.
Yet how much room for memory there is
In the loose girdle of soft rain.

There is even room enough
For the letters of my mother's mother,
Elizabeth,
That have been pressed so long
Into a corner of the roof
That they are brown and soft,
And liable to melt as snow.

Over the greatness of such space
Steps must be gentle.
It is all hung by an invisible white hair.
It trembles as birch limbs webbing the air.

And I ask myself:

"Are your fingers long enough to play
Old keys that are but echoes:
Is the silence strong enough
To carry back the music to its source
And back to you again
As though to her?"

Yet I would lead my grandmother by the hand
Through much of what she would not under-
　　　stand;
And so I stumble. And the rain continues on the
　　　roof
With such a sound of gently pitying laughter.

Hart Crane

Biographical note. Harold Hart Crane was born in Garretsville, Ohio, on July 21, 1899. His parents' marriage broke up in 1916, and he was sent to live with his maternal grandmother. Crane led a nomadic existence, moving restlessly between New York City, Akron, Washington, D.C., and Cleveland. He held various jobs for brief periods as an advertising copywriter, and assisted in his father's candy business, all the time writing poems at night. In 1923 he began work on his great epic, "The Bridge." Years following he lived—supported by generous friends and benefactors— in upstate New York, Europe, and the Caribbean. *White Buildings*, his first book of poems, was published in 1926. In 1931 he received a Guggenheim fellowship and moved to Mexico. On the morning of April 26, 1932, he leaped from the stern of a ship en route from Vera Cruz to New York City. His body was lost at sea.

Hart Crane wrote "My Grandmother's Love Letters" when he was twenty years old. He said of it: "I don't want to make the dear old lady too sweet or too naughty, and balancing on the fine line between these two qualities is going to be fun."

Commentary. It is difficult to imagine this poem saying what it does in any other medium; except, perhaps, music. It sets a melancholy and magical mood immediately. On a rainy evening, a young man struggles on the brink of discovering secrets. Will he take the chance? Gentle, urgent tension— something desired and unresolved—is sustained through the poem. He tests his will, confiding directly in us, and later, to himself.

But if we concentrate too fixedly upon meaning, the poem slips away from us. The mere words in combination are evocative: The mention of *rain* alone sets off a series of associations. He makes up an impossible situation for himself and then tries to overcome it as a poem. Thus we leave him, waiting and wondering.

---

1. Introduction. (Write the following words on the board, to be explained later; and the concept/theme words for class.)

> liable (line 11)
> webbing (line 15)
> pitying (line 26)

> Earliest memory
> How do poems look?
> Form: line
>   stanza

I'm going to read to you a poem by Hart Crane called "My Grandmother's Love Letters." There are a few words you might not understand, but we'll talk about them afterward. Right now, I just want you to listen carefully.

(Mention here any of your own thoughts on the poem, biographical information, and commentary as needed.)

2. Teacher reads poem aloud. (Then, define and discuss the three words listed. It helps to ask for definitions from the class *first*. See what results. Try to keep the children in the context of the poem.)

liable: There's the possibility that the letters might "melt" from being exposed for so long to the elements and dampness in the attic. The letters are susceptible, vulnerable, unprotected.

webbing: The interlacing network of small, thin branches makes him realize how delicate the whole situation is right now.

pitying: feeling sorry for, with tenderness

(Someone might raise the point that *rain* can't feel sorry for anyone! Which is indeed true, and we will get to that later on.)

3. Children read poem aloud.

4. Questions. How do you feel, now that you've heard me read the poem and you've read it yourselves a few times? Happy or sad? Why?

Is this a boy or girl speaking? How do you know? Does it make any difference?

What sort of mood is this person in? What words or expressions tell you his mood?

Can rain "pity" someone, as he says at the end of the poem? Does the rain feel sorry for him, or does he feel sorry for *himself*? Why?

Where is he, anyway? How did he get there? What is he about to do, and why is he afraid?

What might happen to him if he did do it?

If he did open the letters, would he be able to read them?

Is his grandmother dead or alive? How do you know?

20

What might he discover if he did open those letters? What kind of letters are they, do you think? Are they *to* her or *from* her?

What are the "keys" he talks about? What sort of "music" is it?

Put yourself in his shoes: what would *you* do, and why?

(This last question invariably gets a debate going in class between the "letter-openers" and the "letter-leavers." There is an ambiguous feeling about almost everything in the poem, but it doesn't leave the children feeling frustrated, probably because the boy is someone they can identify with, or sympathize with.)

5. The poetic concept. (Ask someone in class to lend you a book of stories or a novel. Hold the two books up in front of you: prose in one hand; this book, with the poem facing the class, in the other. Ask the children to look at the insides of the two books, and to compare them. Don't concentrate on what the words *say* anymore, just on how they *look*.)

How do poems look, compared to stories or a novel?

(Possible answers: The poems are skinnier. They don't go all the way across the page. There's more writing on the page in the novel. There's more space around the words in the poem. The poem is split up into more little parts.)

(Draw two large squares on the board. Over one square, write the word "story." Over the other, write the word "poem." Draw straight parallel lines, imitating a page from each. Take care that the "story" page has even margins, and a few paragraphs indented slightly. The "poem" page should have several, clearly noticeable stanzas composed of lines of varying lengths.)

Why do writers of *stories* use paragraphs? How do we know when a paragraph begins and ends? Why do we use paragraphs when we write?

(Possible answers: The author wants to try a new idea. Someone else is speaking. He indents to show where a paragraph starts. To keep the story from looking like one long sentence.)

Now, what about a *poem*? How do we show a new idea, or a new thought, when we are writing a poem?

(The analogy is apparent. In writing poems, we'll skip a line between stanzas—remember, you've already written the word "stanza" on the board—to show that we are changing to a new idea or a new thought. Furthermore, instead of beginning each new sentence or phrase in our poem right after the preceding one, we'll start a *new line*. The children can begin by perceiving poems as condensed narratives.)

When we are writing stories, we divide them up into sentences, and groups of sentences form paragraphs. When we are writing poems, we divide them into lines, and groups of lines form *stanzas*.

(The line is the basic unit, the "building block" for the poem. We begin by encouraging the children to think one line at a time, thereby to *organize* their thoughts bit by bit.)

6. What we will write about. (The past lives inside us. As adults, we know this in a more habitual way than children do. We reminisce more, because there's a denser fabric of events to turn to. Some memories are vague shadows, others remain—and will remain—etched firmly. What better place to begin, than as close to the beginning as possible?)

What is the *earliest memory* you can think of, the first thing you can ever remember happening to you? Imagine that your mind is a giant wheel, spinning back and back through time. Close your eyes. Look into your *mind's eye*. Where are you? What are you doing? Who else is there with you? This has to be something *you* remember happening, not something that was told to you. Count the years as they pass backwards in your mind, until you can go no further.

(Speak slowly. Pause between each sentence. Give the children time to think deeply, to think slowly.)

7. Children's poems from the book.

8. Reread poem, restate task. Remember, I want you to put each new sentence on a new line; and skip a line between stanzas when you have a new idea. Remember, this should be the very earliest memory you can think of; the first thing you can ever remember happening to you.

9. Writing.

10. Reading aloud. (Time permitting. This lesson ties into the next one, so do not be concerned if there is overlapping. We do not, under any circumstances, want to raise too many issues in any given class; the problem of form [as shape] has an additional dimension [rhyme and rhythm], requiring a separate, but related, discussion.)

My Earliest Memory

My earliest memory was
The time I learned to read
The way I tried to learn
The way I bugged my mother
The way I bugged my father
They always told me to wait a minute
I would wait and wait
And soon my mother came
She carried three books in her hand
And told me to start to read
I read all three of the books
She said that I'd be smart
Because I had not started school
She told me I was reading
On a fourth-grade level

My mother was right
She said I'd be smart
And that is my earliest memory

Cheryl, grade 6

A memory

the light blue room
with the curtains apart
envelops the boy
with very warm sunshine
and he sits with an older sister
who talks—
the t.v. talks
the boy sits there in the light blue sun
the lone ranger jumps on trigger
the 3 stooges hit each other
soupy sales gets a pie in the face—
the sister talks
the boy sits in the light blue room

Joe, grade 8

A Trip to Europe

I remember Europe well
the sight, the sound, sometimes smell
These are things that happened to me
I remember that I was three:

dragging sticks along a fence
a Mother's Day parade I thought all for Momma
a circus for my birthday
Seeing the Eiffel Tower, a flower clock
riding on a boat.

Seeing bears in Berne
Spaghetti in a Brussels square
Holland cheese market
choosing postcards
art museum
Copenhagen
A beautiful boat ride in Norway
Castles
Flamingo Dancers.

These are things that happened to me.
I remember, I was three.

Maria, grade 5

Going up the road
you come to a dead end sign
You keep on going
up the dirt road,
you come to Floyd's pond
I remember in winter
skating on the pond
hockey too
with all the kids
I come out of my daydream
with the movement of the ducks
they are coming up to me
looking for food

I see a fish jump
out in the middle
As I move on
up the pipeline
I remember winter again
sledding and tobogganing down the hill
Having to stop before the ditch
then turning and going back up
I look around and see
a fox dart across the pipeline
I turn around
and go back down the road
remembering when the road
was only half as long
with fields holding
all sorts of adventures
and mysteries
      memories

Donna, grade 6

Speaking to memory

Two Memories

Did you exist, ever?
Did I ride on your shoulders,
did you rock me as I slept?
I know you were tall and carried the weight
of three wives. And though you left us,
your blood is mine.

I have been given this memory.
The cabin where your father lived, leaning wood
on the high bank of the Mississippi.
The slope rotting into water.

Inside, two rooms divided by fireplace
for heat, mantel burdened with bibles
and faded pictures of thirteen children.
He was a godly man, my mother says,
who took a Cherokee wife.

I remember the smell of darkness,
remember my sleep
with animals under the handmade floor,
the stone foundation grunting and the wind
finding the spaces between the boards.
You were there, but I see my grandfather.
And though I open the memory wider,
your face and body merge gently into his.
He is pouring molasses
the color of the winter river on a plate
of biscuits, and the cold
stands stiff inside me.

Cleopatra Mathis

Biographical note. Cleopatra Mathis was born in 1947 in Ruston, Louisiana. She received an MFA in writing from Columbia University. She now lives in Trenton, New Jersey. She tells us, "I began this poem by trying to write about my paternal grandfather, who I saw only a few times before he died. One of the earliest memories I have involves a visit to the old cabin he lived in. That is also one of the few memories I have of my father, who left when I was five and a half years old. The more I tried to write about my grandfather, the more I realized that the poem was really trying to be about my father, and his subsequent absence from my life. I wanted to remember my father and I couldn't. Finally, I addressed my father in the poem, as if I had him in front of me. I asked if he remembered taking care of me, "rocking me as I slept," etc. Then I spoke about the things about the visit I *did* remember: sleeping in that old cabin in the back of the Mississippi River, hearing the animals (pigs, chickens, dogs) grunting under the floor (which was raised off the ground by bricks, so the house wouldn't be flooded in the spring), and that strange breakfast my granddaddy cooked for us the next morning."

Commentary. In "My Grandmother's Love Letters," a young man leaps over a generation; here, the search for her father leads a young woman to her grandfather. When we set our sights on the past, we take a gamble; will it yield riches, or seem impoverished? She's a brave poet, deciding to pursue a memory as far as she can, out of those doubts and conflicts that are so often the sources for poetry. Her habitual attention to detail allows her to summon up certain things in an environment long since gone, as she follows the trail with increasing difficulty.

She feels the lack of balance brought about by the loss of her father and the closeness she feels with her grandfather. And yet, she's oddly unfulfilled, despite the fact she has found something to hold on to, a memory of long ago.

(You might wish to begin by having the children read aloud from work done during the previous lesson, to provide transition.)

1. Introduction. (Write the following words on the board, to be explained later; and the theme words for class.)

> exist (line 1)
> mantel (line 12)
> Earliest memory
> speaking to someone
> rhyme
> rhythm

You remember (yesterday, or whenever the previous lesson occurred) we read a poem by a young man, about his grandmother. This one is called "Two Memories," and it's by Cleopatra Mathis. She is thinking about her father and grandfather. There are two words in the poem you might not understand, but we will talk about them afterward. Right now, I just want you to listen carefully.

(Mention here any of your own thoughts on the poem, biographical information, and commentary as needed.)

2. Teacher reads poem aloud. (Then, define and discuss the two words listed. It helps to ask for definitions from the class *first*. See what results. Try to keep the children's answers in the context of the poem.)

exist: to be; to continue to be; to live

(Of course we know that she did have a father. The sadness of the question comes from the possibility that she hardly knew him, and therefore, has to wonder so deeply about him.)

mantel: a shelf above the fireplace

(In the home she remembers, as in many old homes today, the fireplace is a central focal point. She can see it vividly, and it brings images of her ancestors to mind.)

3. Children read poem aloud.

4. Questions. How do you feel, now that you've heard me read the poem and you've read it yourselves a few times? How does the poem make you feel?

What sort of mood is the poet in? What words or expressions tell you her mood?

To whom is she speaking? How do you know?

What kind of a person do you think her father was? Why?

Why does she say, "I have been *given* this memory?"

Describe the kind of place her grandfather lived in. Do you think she liked being there?

What time of year did she visit her grandfather?
How do you know?

Do you think she feels closer to her father or to her grandfather?

What sort of memories do *you* have of people you've known while growing up, who have been important to you?

What have they taught you that you will always remember?

5. The poetic concept. What is "*rhyme*"? Must we always have it in poetry?

(Again, initiate the discussion by asking the children first. It should be clear by now to everyone that a poem can still be a poem without rhyming at the end of each line in the traditional sense. This doesn't mean that rhyme is "bad," or undesirable, and to be avoided. Rather, if the children are writing along smoothly, and have to stop to think of rhyming words in order to fit their thoughts into rhymed patterns, they will have a tendency to lose momentum, fall into sing-song, "cute" diction, and even distort the meaning and syntax of their writing.

Rhyme is more easily thought of as *the repetition of similar sounds* within the poem's natural structure. Point out the following sound patterns to the children by reading the passages aloud, emphasizing the words indicated:)

I . . . wives . . . mine (lines 4, 5, and 6)

heat . . . thirteen . . . Cherokee . . . sleep (lines 11, 12, 15, and 17)

floor . . . boards . . . pouring (lines 18, 20, and 24)

(Remind the class:) If you find yourself using

words in your poems with sounds that rhyme, good. But don't try too hard to make rhymes, or you'll end up changing your ideas.

What is "*rhythm*"?

What is rhythm in poetry?

What do we mean by rhythm in *music*?

(Wait for answers from the children.)

Rhythm is the *beat*. Natural, everyday talking has a rhythm to it. Everyone's way of talking is different. No two people in the world express themselves the same way—even if they use the same words. You can *feel* the rhythm in the first three lines of the poem. (Read:)

Did you exist, ever?

Did I ride on your shoulders,

did you rock me as I slept?

Rhythm isn't something we have to add to our writing, like a secret ingredient. It's already there. It's a pattern of beats, the way rhyme is a pattern of sounds, just like in music.

6. What we will write about. Last time we wrote down the earliest memories we could think of, the first thing we could ever remember happening to us. Today, we're going to describe a memory again. But this time, I want you to think back to someone you knew when you were much younger—and might still know today. Someone who was important to you, and who taught you something or who was an example to you of the kind of person you want to be. And I want you to *talk to* that person on paper, write the poem as if you were talking to him or her, the way Cleopatra Mathis talks to her father.

7. (Skip step 7 this time, and go right into another reading of the poem.)

8. Reread poem; restate task. Remember, just the way we did last time, you should try to put each new sentence on a new line; and skip a line between stanzas when you have a new idea.

And don't worry about making the lines rhyme. Just write as if you were talking to that person. I want to know who the person is, or was, and what was special about him or her. What did you *learn* from this person?

9. Writing.

10. Reading aloud.

Myth and fantasy

How the Animals Chose Their Places
(A Northern Paiute myth, after Isabel Kelly)

In the old time Coyote was boss.
Coyote said, "Bear, you better stay in the
mountains."
Deer said, "I want to go live in the mountains too!"
Whitefish said, "I want some water."
Duck said he wanted water too.
Swan said, "Look at me, I am growing pretty now;
see, I am white all over."
Bear pounded the ground.
"Ground," he said, "who is talking about me?"
Ground said, "Indian talks pretty mean,"
so Bear went out and bit him.
"I want to stay here in the rocks,"
said Mountain Sheep.
"I like to feel the ground," Rock said,
"I like to stay here in one place and not move."
Sagebrush said he felt the same way.
This is Coyote's story.

Jarold Ramsey

Biographical note. Jarold Ramsey tells us, "I grew up on a ranch in Central Oregon, just across the Deschutes River from the Reservation of the Confederated Warm Springs Tribes, and went all through school with Indian kids, including Wasco Chinookans, Warm Springs Sahaptins, and Northern Paiutes. But it never occurred to me that my Indian friends and their families might still be associated with traditional oral literatures of great wisdom and beauty. Not until I'd moved to New York State, with its self-conscious Indian heritage, did I begin to wake up to my own, as an Oregonian. I began to ransack libraries, I pestered old Indian friends, and now, a decade later, I feel I've only *begun*."

" 'How the Animals Chose Their Places' is one of a series of verse adaptations or workings I made around 1971 from Oregon Indian songs and myths. What seemed to come through was a wonderfully playful, wild, childlike and yet wise force of imagination, as if the high desert world of the Northern Paiutes were telling its own story in a spirit of sacred amusement. As always with true myth (and, I think, with the greatest poetry), everything contributes its crucial part to the great real statement: This is the way it is.

"I cherish this poem, because in working over its original, I first felt some confidence in my ability to render the mythic gaiety and keenness of such texts. Once you understand what's going on, then *of course* this is how the Paiute animals set up their habitats. *Of course* Coyote was boss then; of course Swan chose to grow pretty—and vain; naturally

37

Ground heard everything; and (my own favorite) naturally Rock and his neighbor Sagebrush wanted only to 'stay in one place and not move.'

"An old Paiute shaman named Sam Wata once wondered out loud about a possible connection between our Anglo exploitation of his country, and our utter indifference to his myths and beliefs: 'Maybe white people don't know about the beginning of this earth.'

"I'd like to hope that Sam Wata might recognize 'How the Animals Chose Their Places' as one of the stories telling that sacred beginning."

Commentary. We read myths to preserve a sense of wonder in a world where more and more is taken for granted. Whether we actually believe them or not has to be irrelevant. This refreshingly basic reworking of an ancient native American story carries us back to a time before time, to the very beginnings of things, when not only things, but facts (death, evil, the nature of humans and animals) were established.

I've always liked the gentle irony of the poem. Coyote may have been "boss," or king of beasts; but his first command to Bear sets off a chain reaction of responses from the other animate and inanimate subjects, quite insistent from the beginning about where they want to be, and what they'll do there.

A sense of place is important to all of us.

---

1. Introduction. (Write these two words on the board, to be explained later.)

myth (in sub-title of the poem; also the
    subject of today's discussions)
Sagebrush (line 16)

(A map of the United States might also be helpful
in this lesson, so that you can point out the location
of the two states mentioned, should they be unfamiliar to the children.)

Today we're going even *further* back in time. I'm
going to read you a myth from the Paiute tribe of
Southwestern Utah (indicate on map if necessary).
It's called "How the Animals Chose Their Places,"
and it was adapted by the poet Jarold Ramsey. Then
we will talk about the two words I've written on the
blackboard. Right now, I just want you to listen
carefully.

(Mention here any of your own thoughts on the
poem, biographical information, and commentary
as needed.)

2. Teacher reads poem aloud. (Then, define
and discuss the two words listed. It helps to ask for
definitions from the class *first*. See what results. Try
to keep the children in the context of the poem.)

myth: an invented (made-up) story or poem that
    explains some belief, way of life, or how some-
    thing came to be. We usually don't know how
    or when a myth actually began, or who wrote
    it.

sagebrush: a white or gray low-lying shrub (bush)
    found on the Western plains and deserts. It is
    the state flower of Nevada (indicate on map if
    necessary).

3. Children read poem aloud.

39

4. Questions. How do you feel, now that you've heard me read the poem and you've read it yourselves a few times? How does the poem make you feel?

"In the old time Coyote was boss." Let's talk about "the old time." That was a long, long time ago. What do you think America was like back then, when these events took place?

Was Coyote *really* the boss? What does a boss do? Are the other animals paying attention to him? How do you know?

Can animals *really* talk to each other? How do animals communicate? Can a dog communicate with another dog? Give me some examples of animals communicating with each other, or with people.

What do the different animals want, and why? (Go down the list.)

Why do you think this myth was invented?

What does it explain? (This leads into the discussion below.)

5. The poetic theme. How many people in class believe that what is described in the poem is *true;* that it really happened? (Obviously, most of the children won't believe it.)

But do we *have* to believe it, in order to enjoy it?

Are myths the same in all countries?

Do we have any myths in America today?

What are some of the things you *used* to believe were true, when you were younger, that you don't believe *now*?

(You might begin a cumulative list on the board,

and add to it as ideas and remembered "myths" are called out, headed "I used to believe that. . . ." We want to work toward an awareness that many things we believe to be true at different times in our lives do not always remain so; this is a place where you the teacher, as an adult, can make an unusually important contribution. Being older, you have a different perspective on childhood, and should try to talk about some of your changing beliefs, as they relate to the question. After a few minutes of discussion, point to the list you've assembled on the board.)

Are *these* myths?

(We see that myths can exist on a broad cultural, even anthropological, level, of course; but just as validly, on a very personal, individual level—in the lives of your students. We want to lay the groundwork for writing about *both* true and made-up subjects in a poem. The lesson in the following chapter, on dreams, extends this principle.)

6. What we will write about. Today, we are going to make up a memory. We are going to write our *own* myths.

You have several choices. You can put yourself into an *imaginary* (made-up) *land*, and tell us what it's like there, how the people live, what they look like, and so on. Or, you can pick *anything* in the world: a thing, an animal, a place, and write about how it *came to be*. Or, you might like to take one of those myths from when you were younger, and write about it more fully: how you first came to believe it; who taught it to you; when you found out that it wasn't true.

7. Children's poems from the book. (These particular examples should be very helpful in getting the children started.)

8. Reread poem; restate task. Remember, just as we have already learned, you want to put each new sentence on a new line; and skip a line between stanzas when you have a new idea. And don't worry about making the lines rhyme.

(Repeat the instructions from step 6, and make sure that the children see what their choices are. Perhaps several of them want to *combine* the choices, which would be fine and acceptable.)

9. Writing.

10. Reading aloud.

The Andromedia

In the mist of darkness
A creature on all legs stopped me.
"Go no further," said the creature.
"Why," said I.
"Because you shall miss the gold in the cave,"
     said he.
"I want the gold, where is it," said I.
He took me to the end of the cave,
But there was nothing there!
He said, "The gold is in your soul,
     and I want it."
Then he changed his shape.
He had a horn on his forehead.
Then there was a flash of light,
     and he said "Nevermore."
After this there was a flash of light
     and smoke, and he was gone.

I went back to the trail and it was morning
In a place of never ending heat
and mist of a day.

William, grade 4

Stuffed Animal Land

I wonder if there's a stuffed
Animal Land
with little munchkins
running about, gathering
stuffing, materials, pins, threads, and buttons.

All different figures, colors,
and types.

Some stuffed bears, dogs, cats,
ducks, elephants, etc.
I'd really love to be there
No matter what animal you want
it would be there

You call it impossible
But it may be true!

Sheila, grade 4

How the Sky Came to Be

The sky came to be
by marshmallows bursting in the air.

The sky came to be
with crayons coloring it blue.

The sky came to be
with clouds of whipped cream in the air.

The sky came to be
with a gigantic blue balloon covering
    the whole world.

The sky came to be
to light up the whole world.

The sky came to be
so we could see.

Miriam, grade 5

Dreams

Dream Take: 22

Same old Mexico Lisbon set
rainy at night & shimmery.
I alone flop around at midnight,
see everything from angel angle.

New moonless couples mourn by
arm in arm & all hands
after evenings of being quiet,
for soon whatever's to happen's

happened already, always has.
I smile out over the situation
to keep their tears to myself,
tired of time & so much in need of

this mirage of lovers parading.
Safe, I can sense that I'm soon to
awake with no possible camera
to record what I just saw asleep.

Al Young

Biographical note. Al Young was born in 1939 in Ocean Springs, Mississippi, grew up around the South and in Detroit, and now lives in Palo Alto, California. He writes, "As I recall, 'Dream Take: 22' got written in the very mid-sixties during the period when I was meditating and keeping a fitful sort of dream journal. Having noticed our tendency to 'straighten' or 'fix up' dreams in the telling, I tried to scribble mine down directly from memory while they were still fresh and clear with all their ragged craziness intact. I was learning how dreams—like stories, poems, music, and waking experiences—were self-contained, suspended in a logic, rhythm, and meaning all their own. One night in a dream, I found myself present in a place that was Portugal and Mexico rolled into one; countries where I had recently travelled. Everything that takes place in the poem took place in the dream with all of its pictorial feelings. Oddly, though, I felt grandly aloof. It was as if I were an invisible spectator whose spirit was projecting all that I saw and felt. Thus was I given to see what mystics might mean when they speak of creation (the universe itself) being like a gigantic dream or movie, if you will, in which we each play enormous roles and yet, because we are free to write our own parts as we go along, we also help to create the dream while delighting in its mysterious 'realness.'

"The poem grew out of just such dreaming and imagining. It was simply one of those magical insights that I feel lucky to have experienced in this way, and even luckier to have jotted down."

Commentary. This poem conveys the odd logic of dreams, where events continue to happen, but not quite in the same manner as they do in real life. The "logic" comes across through the simple device of arranging the poem in four stanzas of four lines each, in direct contradiction to the narrator's shifting perspective. He shows himself to be the dreamer, first from outside and above; then, from within himself; and then from the brink of wakefulness, reassured by the promise of forgetfulness.

Familiarity—that it is a recurrent experience ("Take 22")—and uniqueness coexist. He's had this *feeling* before, but the dream about loneliness is always different. Al Young has the knack, here and elsewhere in his poetry, of being able to fuse what's real with what's imagined.

---

1. **Introduction.** (Write these four words on the board, to be explained later; and off to the side, as shown, the theme for today's class.)

Lisbon (line 1)	dreams
shimmery (line 2)	
mourn (line 5)	
mirage (line 13)	

(A map of the world might also be helpful in this lesson, so that you can point out the locations of Mexico and Lisbon, as the distance between them is important toward an understanding of the poem.)

Today we're going to talk and write about a subject that everyone in the world knows something about: dreams. All of us dream every night, often three times a night or even more. Here's a poem by Al Young called "Dream Take: 22." First, I will read it to you, then we'll discuss the four words I've written on the board. Listen carefully. It's a very mysterious poem! (Mention here any of your own thoughts on the poem, biographical information, and commentary, as needed.)

2. Teacher reads poem aloud. (Then, define and discuss the four words listed. It helps to ask for definitions from the class *first*. See what results. Try to keep the vocabulary in the context of the poem.)

Lisbon: (indicate on map) the capital of Portugal; a seaport city

shimmery: to shine with a trembling light. Perhaps the rain makes the streets shine as cars pass, and under the streetlights the pavement shimmers and gleams.

mourn: to grieve, to be sad and sorrowful when someone dies. He uses the word in an odd way in the poem. It could be to help maintain the image of darkness under the cloudy sky, the rain, the new moon (i.e., no moon).

mirage: We usually think of seeing a mirage in the desert, the sight of water in the distance, which is actually a layer of hot air reflecting downward upon the sand. Here, he might mean the illusion of people where in fact there are none, as "it is only a dream." He wants to see the lovers so much that he creates them, out of nothingness.

3. Children read poem aloud.

4. Questions. How do you feel, now that you've heard me read the poem and you've read it yourselves a few times? How does the poem make you feel?

Is he enjoying himself? What do you think *his* mood is, and why?

Where is he? Where is Mexico? Where is Lisbon (use map to show the separation)? How can he put them together the way he does? (Establishing the point that almost anything can happen in a dream.)

Is he by himself? How do you know?

What does "angel angle" mean?

What does he see that makes him feel lonelier?

How can he smile if he feels so alone and lonely?

What kind of "camera" is he talking about at the end? Is it a *real* camera? (Or could it be his own mind, his imagination, his thoughts; and his fear that he won't remember his dream when he awakens?)

5. The poetic theme. (Dreams can be a very fertile area for poetry writing ideas. The dreams of childhood are often vivid, colorful, even terrifying—as they cross over into nightmares.

You can help the children who say they have difficulty remembering their dreams. Studies in dream retention have shown that if we tell ourselves before we go to sleep at night that we want to remember what we dream, we stand a good chance of doing so.

Some of your more adventurous students might want to start keeping pencil and paper at their bedsides, to jot down dreams when they first awaken, while they are fresh in their minds.

The class discussion should serve to intensify the children's readiness to articulate their dreams as poems.)

Where do you suppose dreams come from? How are they caused? Why do you think we have dreams? How long do your dreams last?

(Make a "Dream List" on the board. Write down catch-phrase responses to the question that follows as they are called out, so that as the list grows, the children see the variety and strangeness possible.)

What is the most incredible dream you've ever had?

(You'll probably get some subtle competition going as the children begin to warm to the subject! But this is an exciting way to develop their interest, and for them to get a glimpse into the imaginations of their classmates.)

What is the difference between a dream and a nightmare?

What is a "daydream"? Does anyone here daydream? Where? About what?

How about a "fantasy"? What is that? Is that different from a dream?

(Dreams can lead to good poems because, as you will notice, in the telling of them, the children invariably exaggerate and embellish details. Writing about dreams gives children unwritten license to stretch their minds.

Behind both dreams and poems lie the same mysterious impulses.)

6. What we will write about. Today, as you can probably guess by now, I'd like you to write down the most incredible dream or nightmare you have ever had. If you wish, you may combine parts of different dreams or nightmares you have had, to make one incredible and fantastic dream.

There's only one rule. I don't want you to use the word "dream" anywhere in the poem, or to say, "I dreamed that . . ." or "But when I woke up, it was only a dream," or to use any expression that tells us it was a dream. Why? Because, if you don't mention "dream," it will come out sounding more like an incredible—maybe true—story.

So just start right in, telling us what happened with as much detail as possible. I want to be able to *see* this dream come to life!

7. Children's poems from the book.

8. Reread poem; restate task. Remember, as I've mentioned to you before, you want to put each new sentence on a new line; and skip a line between *stanzas* when you have a new idea, when you come to another part of the dream. And don't worry about making the lines rhyme.

(Repeat the instructions from step 6, just to make sure that the children understand not to use the word "dream.")

9. Writing.

10. Reading aloud. This lesson will most probably go beyond the usual time period. You may find you only have time for reading and discussion. It is certainly appropriate to ask the children to write the poem at home over the next day or two. You might even ask them to try the dream retention exercise that night, then ask them the next day if it worked.

The Strange Dream

I am running
  not far behind
    is a man
    who looks
    exactly like
    my father
yet I know it's
    not him
for he is somewhere else
and I've got to find him

I pass through a restaurant
    and a garden
    filled with green and red
    huge bursting flowers
    blocking my way
    filling up the place where
    the dead end used to be
    and the man is laughing

Now I'm in the car with
    the family and
we're pulling a trailer
    and I think "How strange"

We pass under a bridge but
the trailer flies over it
and I think "How strange"

Sharon, grade 7

Clouds

I walked inside a cloud
a darkness I picked it up
without falling.

But it rained on me.
I decided to go to bed
I fell asleep and thought
about what had happened.

Pam, grade 4

Blobs of numbers

I was sleeping and fidgety
It was raining
I didn't feel too good
I dozed off
I thought I was staring at the shutters
on my bedroom window
All of a sudden they turned into numbers
It was scary
I remember the numbers 4 and 8
They started marching
I could even hear the marching sounds
stamp, stamp, stamp
Then I heard a whistle and they all
pulled out swords and came at me
They started chanting
Blob, blob, blob, blob, blob
It got louder and louder
and big clumps of clay hovered over my head
and started covering my feet
I couldn't move
The numbers were coming closer and closer

Pam, grade 7

Part II
Sharpening
the Senses

See and hear

I Stand and Look

I stand and look in the dark under a cloud,
But I see in the distance where the sun shines,
I see the thin haze on the tall white steeples of
    the city,
I see the glistening of the waters in the distance.

Walt Whitman

Biographical note. Walt Whitman was born in West Hills (Long Island), New York, in 1819. As a young man, he held a variety of odd jobs in and around the New York area: working in printing offices, where he learned the trade; becoming a schoolteacher at age seventeen; then a journalist. From 1846-47, he was editor of the Brooklyn *Daily Eagle*.

In 1855, he published his great book of poems, *Leaves of Grass*, in an edition of 1,000 copies, which he typeset and distributed himself. Very few copies were sold, but one found its way into the hands of Ralph Waldo Emerson—who, some years earlier, had complained that America still had no "ideal poet." Emerson was immediately taken by the book: "I find it the most extraordinary piece of wit and wisdom that America has yet contributed . . . I greet you at the beginning of a great career," he wrote enthusiastically to the young poet.

During the Civil War, Whitman worked as a wound dresser, not serving in combat, but administering to the disabled. Some of his most moving poetry came out of this experience.

Whitman's major collection of essays, *Democratic Vistas*, in which he spelled out his theories of poetry, was published in 1871, along with a fifth edition of *Leaves of Grass*. He died in Camden, New Jersey, in 1892.

His poetry signalled the first true break with the more formal verse tradition of England, which had had such an important influence on American poetry up to that time. By answering Emerson's call, Whitman became the exemplary American poet of the age.

Commentary. We turn to the poems of Walt Whitman expecting to find ecstatic diction and an inexhaustible tide of language—celebrations of all life. As you see here, his work also has a more intimate, lyrical quality. These brief glimpses are building blocks for his best-known epics.

Reading such a short, condensed poem, there may be a tendency to look for more than just what we find. Is the poem *only about* a man standing on a hillside in temporary darkness, looking off to a distant, shining scene? Or is he saying something "symbolic" about "hope" and "optimism"?

Obviously, no single answer is even possible. More immediately, we can say how powerful and clear the images are: like a black-and-white snapshot, instantaneous and lasting.

Even within the constraints of four lines, Whitman is the poet of affirmation.

---

1. Introduction. (A poet needs a good set of eyes and ears, and needs to know how to use them. Throughout the book, we emphasize the importance of good listening. These next two lessons focus upon the basics of *image* and its natural extension, *imagination*. We'll try to start the children thinking about how to communicate visually through written words, in their poetry.)

(Write these two words on the board, to be explained later; and off to the side, as shown, the theme words for today's class.)

haze (line 3)	image
glistening (line 4)	describe

Today we're going to hear a very short poem, only four lines, by one of the most famous American poets, Walt Whitman. It's called "I Stand and Look." But even though it is short, it says a lot, and will give you much to think about. While I am reading the poem to you, I'd like you to close your eyes and try to *see* what he is describing. Then, we will discuss the words I've written on the board.

(Mention here any of your own thoughts on the poem, biographical information, and commentary, as needed.)

2. Teacher reads poem aloud. (Then, define and discuss the two words listed. It helps to ask for definitions from the class *first*. See what results. Try to keep the children in the context of the poem.)

haze: a light cloud of moisture or smoke in the air, usually caused by dust or heat (It could certainly be a warm, summer afternoon in the poem.)

glistening: sparkling, shining brightly (In this case, the reflection of the sun on the water.)

3. Children read poem aloud.

4. and 5. Questions; the poetic concept. (We're combining these two steps, because the poem is so short, and too much discussion will take away from its impact.)

How do you feel, now that you've heard me read the poem and you've read it yourselves a few times? How does the poem make you feel?

When I read the poem to you, and asked you to close your eyes, what did you *see*? What does the poem describe? (You'll have a variety of answers, leading into the next question.)

What do I mean by *describe*? (Point to word on the blackboard.) When we describe something, we're using words to tell other people about it, so that they can see it or understand it also.

When you hear this poem, you *see* certain things in your mind. You see the image of a cloud, the image of a church steeple, the image of shining water. What is an *image*? (Again, point to blackboard.)

An image is *a picture made by using words.* An image is what happens when we describe something so well that we can *see* it, even though it isn't there. Those of you who draw or paint are making a different kind of image. How are you doing that? (Wait for answers from the children.) You're using pencils or crayons or watercolors to make pictures. When we write poetry, or any kind of writing, we try to use words the same way—to make a picture. Many people think it's much harder to do this with words than with pencils or crayons or paint! What do you think?

How does Walt Whitman make us *see* what he is *describing*? (Wait for answers from the class.)

He uses very simple words that everyone can understand. He makes it very clear to us where he is, and what he is doing, because he wants to *share* his images.

And in each line, he puts a *different image*.
    (Write on board: cloud
                    sun
                    haze on steeples
                    glistening waters
Read the poem to the class again, placing emphasis on these four images.)

6. What we will write about. I'd like you to imagine yourself being in a place you know well, and where you have been, for example, looking out of your bedroom window, or standing at the shore of the beach or, like Walt Whitman, on a hillside or in the park. And then, once you picture yourself at that familiar place, I would like you to describe what you see when you look around. I would like you to make images of what you see—so clear that when the rest of us in class hear or read your poem, we'll be able to see just what you see.

7. Children's poems from the book.

8. Reread poem, restate task. Remember to put a new sentence on a new line; and skip a line between stanzas when you have a new idea, when you come to another part of the description. Don't worry about making the lines rhyme.

And remember to make your images very clear, so that *we* will be able to see what *you* see.

9. Writing.

10. Reading aloud. (When the children read their poems, you might ask the others to close their eyes and try to visualize what is being described.

62

For example, if it's tree, what kind of tree; or if it's a group of buildings outside a window, how tall they are, what color, etc. Then they can measure their images against the intent of the poet. This is an exercise that can involve everyone, whether they are able to write the poem right away or not.)

I saw something
in our cellar.
It looked like an eye
but it was a stove.

Rodney, grade 4

The Sea

Slowly the tide came in
littering the beach with shells.
Foam danced on the top of
the waves.
Fish struggled to keep alive
in tiny pools.
A whale spouted far away.

Coming towards me
was the sea.

Gretchen, grade 5

The smallest thing of all

I'm looking out
the window
of the school

    and I can see
white blackish snow
with brown greenish
grass
       and the lightness
of the day

I can see Mr. Jones
driving away in
his car

I can see tall
grass growing in
the fields
the cars passing by
poster signs

Then I can
see the smallest
thing of all
a robin
whistling alone

Tom, grade 8

Image

The Singer

Crackle and flash almost in the kitchen sink—the
thunderclap follows even as I
jump back frightened,
afraid to touch metal—

    The roofgutters pouring down
      whole rivers, making holes in the earth—
The electric bulbs fade and go out,
   another thin crackling lights the window
and in the instant before the next onslaught of
     kettledrums,

a small bird, I don't even know its name,
among the seagreen tossed leaves
                begins its song.

Denise Levertov

Biographical note. Denise Levertov was born in England in 1923, and came to the U.S. after World War II. She now lives in Massachusetts. She tells us, "This poem tells you something, and that telling *is itself.* It describes a flash of lightning, a clap of thunder, and violent downpour of a summer storm; and in a brief lull of that storm, a small bird, undaunted, is heard singing. I wrote the poem in Maine, in an old farmhouse, probably on the same day as the storm itself—not long after, in any case. I want to remind you that a poem is printed just the way it is for good reasons, if it is well-made—just like the score for a piece of music. So don't try to read this or any other poem too quickly, otherwise its sounds and rhythms will not come through to you."

Commentary. Here's a piece of the poet's experience, no more than a few moments' time during a violent rainstorm, lifted neatly away from the surrounding life and presented to us perfectly crafted. Notice the effortless way she illuminates the scene, lightning and lightbulbs alternating with absolute darkness.

The poet is situated—placed—in specific relation to the world around her, so that when something happens, her response becomes all the more vivid. She begins by portraying herself as irresolute and intimidated in the face of natural events, then emerges buoyed up by the bird's song.

What makes this poem so much more than just a report of something that happened? Her imagination gives each particular detail an extra dimension: the invasion of the house; fear of violation by electric shock; quick shift outside, hemmed in by rushing waters; fear of isolation—all build to the surprising resolution, from oppressive fright to anonymous beauty.

---

1. Introduction. (We have established a firm foundation with image-making; now we move to the mysterious part of our minds that produces those images: the *imagination*. And it is more accurate to talk about what the imagination *does*, how we can make active *use* of it; rather than trying to pin down what it actually *is*.)

(Write these four words on the board, to be explained later; and off to the side, as shown, the theme words for today's class.)

crackle (line 1)	image
roofgutters (line 5)	imagine
onslaught (line 9)	imagination
kettledrums (line 9)	

I'm going to read you a scary poem. But it has a happy ending. It's called "The Singer," by Denise Levertov. If you close your eyes while I'm reading, like we did last time, I know you will be able to see the things she describes so well. Think about the *images* that go through your mind as you listen. Then we will discuss the words I've written on the board.

(Mention here any of your own thoughts on the poem, biographical information, and commentary, as needed.)

2. Teacher reads poem aloud. (Then, define and discuss the four words listed. It helps to ask for definitions from the class *first*. See what results. Try to keep the children in the context of the poem.)

crackle: a sharp, sudden, repeated noise. Lightning is caused (does anyone in the class know how?) by electricity going from one cloud to another, or from a cloud to earth.

roof gutters: a channel or narrow pipe on the edge of the roof that carries running rainwater, or water from melting snow, away to the ground

onslaught: an attack

kettledrums: the large drums in the orchestra made from brass or copper (So the "onslaught of kettledrums" is . . . ?)

3. Children read poem aloud.

4. Questions. How do you feel, now that you've heard me read the poem and you've read it yourselves a few times? How does the poem make you feel?

Compare *her* feelings at the beginning of the poem and at the end. What are they?

Is she in the city or the country? How can you tell?

What part of the house is she in when the storm comes?

Is she afraid? Do you think she is alone in the house?

Describe some of the images you see in the poem. What are "seagreen tossed leaves"?

How would *you* feel if you were there?

5. The poetic concept. (In teaching poetry writing, we want to encourage the most fundamental aspect of a child's imagination: making up pictures in the mind.

Problems occur during the translation of thought into language, which follows image-making; that's the difficult connection. Some children, needless to say, are better at it than others, which will mean that they are better *writers*, not necessarily better *imaginers*. Some children can articulate their imaginings verbally, and will call out all manner of marvelous things—but when it comes to setting them down, they are "blocked."

I encourage you to take dictation from these children whenever possible, to collaborate with them in the poems that are said better than they're written. (See **Taking Dictation,** page 71.)

What qualities can we look for in good image-making? Inventiveness; the ability to bring different ideas together; uniqueness and freshness of language; emotional clarity; alertness; music. But let's remember to be realistic. Not *all* of these things will be in every poem. What you *can* do is keep insisting, as you have all along, that the children try to organize thoughts and ideas more clearly.

This process of organizing a simple succession of images stimulates the search for more and better images—and these in turn grow out of being awake to what's going on in our everyday lives.)

(Point to the series of theme words on the board.)

Let's think back to what we learned last time. What is an *image*? (Make sure they understand and remember, so that the connection is clear.)

Who has an *imagination* in this class? (Wait for a show of hands.) You should *all* have raised your hands.

Where is the imagination located? Is it in a specific part of your brain? (Await replies.) No, it's part of your mind. What does the imagination *do?* (Await replies.)

When you are writing, your imagination is the part of your mind that you are using to think of, or to make up, to *imagine* (point to word on blackboard) good and interesting *images,* good pictures with words.

How many of you think that Denise Levertov, the poet who wrote this poem we just read, has a good imagination? Why?

Because she picked out a piece of her life, of her experience, something that happened to her, and just by using words from her imagination, she showed us what it felt like to be caught in a storm in a little cabin alone in the woods.

And that's the kind of writing I'd like you do today.

6. What we will write about. I'd like *you* to pick out a piece of your life, something exciting or happy or sad or scary or beautiful that happened to you. I'd like you to *describe* it, using your imagination, so that we can *see* what was exciting or happy or sad or scary or beautiful.

Or, those of you who wish to can *make up* something that didn't happen, but that you would like to describe as if it did happen.

7. Children's poems from the book. (After each one, you might ask what feeling they got from hearing it.)

8. Reread poem, restate task. Remember to put a new sentence on a new line; and skip a line between stanzas when you have a new idea. Don't worry about making the lines rhyme. Think about how to make your imagination work for you.

9. Writing.

10. Reading aloud in class. (What feelings do we get when we hear the various poems read?)

TAKING DICTATION

Taking dictation as a lead-in to poetry requires some one-to-one time with those children who are experiencing unusual difficulty setting their thoughts to paper—but who *are* able to articulate them verbally.

Skilled fifth- and sixth-graders and older children can take dictation from very young children. Kindergartners can "write" poems through this simple method.

While the child tells you his poem, write down the words as they come, making slash marks, as shown below, whenever there is a breath pause or the end of a phrase or sentence.

Then, realign the poem so that each breath pause determines the end of one line and the beginning of the next. Here are two examples:

First, the transcription:
Outside
is fun if you like/but if you are not the type/you will

71

not like the outside/but if you have heard other kids talk/about the outside/and you like it/you should go outside/but if you go outside/and do not like it/you should not go outside/anymore

Then, the realignment, according to pauses:

Outside

is fun if you like
but if you are not the type
you will not like the outside
but if you have heard other kids talk
about the outside
and you like it
you should go outside
but if you go outside
and do not like it
you should not go outside
anymore

Andrea, grade 4

A Memory

when I was four year old/my brother and sister/were cooking some french fries/and they put some hot grease on the table/and my father always gave me some coffee/and the grease looked like coffee/and I reached for the hot glass of grease/and it fell on me/and my father took me to the hospital/and they put my body in some ice/the ice was in a rag/they put my feet in a thing of ice/and after that my father

took me to the store/and brought me some ice cream/
and took me home/and I gave all my family some
ice cream

A Memory

when I was four years old
my brother and sister
were cooking some french fries
and they put some hot grease on the table
and my father always gave me some coffee
and the grease looked like coffee
and I reached for the hot glass of grease
and it fell on me
and my father took me to the hospital
and they put my body in some ice
the ice was in a rag
they put my feet in a thing of ice
and after that my father took me to the store
and brought me some ice cream
and took me home
and I gave all my family some ice cream

Chuck, grade 4

I particularly like the irrefutable, direct logic of
Andrea's poem, with its references to what "other
kids" think; and the strong narrative flow of
Chuck's, with its clear beginning, middle, and
end—in which ice is transformed to ice cream!

Moon Light

I lie where the
moon shines on me.
  I hear sad voices
and the trees weeping
at the side of my house,
and the flowers in the
ground have tears to show.

Lorna, grade 7

Darkness

In a graveyard late at night,
An owl screeches,
The darkness kidnaps your soul,
You are pulled away, far, far away into the
    frightening darkness.

Lynn, grade 5

Grass

Green grass waving gayly
in the meadow looks very beautiful,
it looks like it is sweeping
the sky of all bitterness.

Brian, grade 4

Part III
Who Am I?

First impressions

Autobiographia Literaria

When I was a child
I played by myself in a
corner of the schoolyard
all alone.

I hated dolls and I
hated games, animals were
not friendly and birds
flew away.

If anyone was looking
for me I hid behind a
tree and cried out "I am
an orphan."

And here I am, the
center of all beauty!
writing these poems!
Imagine!

Frank O'Hara

Biographical note. Frank O'Hara was born in 1926. He attended Harvard College and the University of Michigan. He moved to New York City in 1951, where he became closely associated with John Ashbery and Kenneth Koch, the "New York poets."

He worked for *Art News*, and at the Museum of Modern Art, for many years in the International Program; and he supervised numerous major exhibitions there.

O'Hara was vitally connected to both the literary and art worlds. He wrote quickly and spontaneously. His best-known collection of work is probably *Lunch Poems* (Pocket Poets Series, City Lights Books, 1964), which were ostensibly just that, written when he could find the time during his busy day.

He died, too soon, in a tragic accident on Fire Island during the summer of 1966. His gravestone reads: "Grace to be born and live as variously as possible."

Commentary. It's entirely appropriate that the title of Frank O'Hara's poem refers back to "Biographia Literaria," in which Coleridge attempted to define the imagination. O'Hara is likewise concerned with the roots of imaginative thought: How is it that some of us grow up to be poets, and others do not?

Beneath these philosophical speculations, however, is a poem of childlike poignancy, a deceptively simple sketch of how the way things used to be, and points out the way things are for the poet.

Frank O'Hara led a sociable, constantly gregarious life; he was equally generous to friends, acquaintances, and people he didn't know, but he was also an extremely private person, as this poem gracefully intimates.

A writer needs to experience both involvements: with society and people, and an introspective engagement with himself.

---

1. Introduction. (John Holt has written, "Everyone is interested in something, if only himself—and usually much more than that." This lesson, and the three following, are designed to help you take the children on a non-self-conscious exploration of themselves through "self-portrait" poems from different points of view.)

(Only one word in the poem should provide any difficulty; and off to the side as shown, write the theme words for today's class.)

orphan (line 12)   image
                      first impressions

Here is a poem by Frank O'Hara called "Autobiographia Literaria." That is Latin for "literary autobiography," the story of a writer's life, exactly what the poem is. But it is a very *short* story, as you will now hear. Then, we will discuss the words I've written on the board.

(Mention here any of your own thoughts on the poem, biographical information, and commentary, as needed.)

2. Teacher reads poem aloud. (Then, define and discuss the word listed. It helps to ask for definitions from the class *first*. See what results. Try to keep the vocabulary in the context of the poem.)

orphan: a child whose parents have both died

3. Children read poem aloud.

4. Questions. How do you feel, now that you've heard me read the poem and you've read it yourselves a few times? How does the poem make you feel?

Let's start from the *end* of the poem this time. What kind of person did he end up to be, and how can you tell?

What kind of life did he have as a child? Was it happy or sad? Did he have any friends? How can you tell from the poem?

Why do you think he played by himself?

Why do *you* sometimes play by yourself instead of with other children?

Why were "animals not friendly" to him?

Who might be "looking for" him?

Why did he want people to think he was an orphan?

How did he end up to be a poet when he got older?

Have you ever looked at an adult and tried to guess what he or she was like as a child? Do you think it is possible to tell?

What kind of person do you think *you'll* be when you are an adult?

What kind of person do you *want* to be?

5. The poetic theme. Remember when we talked about *image* and *imagination*? (Review these concepts once again with the class.) Well, let's talk about what kind of *image* people have when they first meet you. What is their *first impression* of you? (Point to words on the blackboard. Spend some time discussing with children the aspects of themselves that they believe come across upon first meeting someone: physical as well as emotional.)

We often discover, don't we, that after we get to know someone better, as time goes by, the first impression we had can change. It is possible to begin by *not* liking someone, and then you can get to *like* him—or the other way around. Think about someone who is a good friend of yours. What was your *first impression* of that person, when you were just getting to know him or her? And how do you feel about that person now? (Try to elicit some personal anecdotes from the children about their relationships with friends.)

(What we are getting at here is a further extension of developing perception skills, only this time as they relate to the way we look—appear to be—to others.)

6. What we will write about. Imagine for a moment that you are walking down the street, when suddenly you meet *yourself* coming from the other direction!

What does this person look like?

What is he or she wearing?

How tall is he/she?

How is he/she acting?

What is the very *first* impression you have, the

first thing you notice about that person, the first thing that strikes you?

What is the *second* thing you notice about that person?

Then, after you have *described* that person (review this word again), I want you to *guess* at what he/she might be like inside. But remember, it would have to be a first impression guess, because you've never seen him/her before.

You might want to start this poem by saying, "I was walking down the street when I met me for the first time . . ." then go into the descriptions, impressions, and guesses about the person.

7. Children's poems from the book. ("Little Girl Image," especially, should help the children make the connection between image and impression, as they connect in turn with how we describe another person from the *outside*.)

8. Restate task. (Do *not* reread the O'Hara poem in this case, as it was introduced to familiarize the children with a more personal vein of writing, not to exemplify this particular assignment.)

Remember to put a new sentence on a new line; skip a line between stanzas when you have a new idea, or come to a new part of yourself that you are describing, a new impression that you have of yourself.

Think about how to create an *image* of yourself on paper!

9. Writing.

10. Reading aloud in class.

First impressions

Having fun,
Laughing loud,
Though sometimes
Too loud.
Who cares?
It's still joy.

Be concerned.
Reaching out
With a smile
To help a friend.

Loving life,
Loving people,
But having doubts,
Need to straighten them out.
The dumb mistakes
That she makes.
A little crazy,
But still,
Nice.

Is this
What they think
When they meet me
And greet me
And ask how I've been.

Anne, grade 9

Little Girl Image

This was my big day.
There I stand in the door
Having my picture taken
With a fake smile
For today I began school

I was going to miss watching my TV
Sleeping in late
I was going to miss my little girl image

But there I stand awaiting the big day
Yet I don't want to go for now
For now my little girl image is starting
to disappear.

Colette, grade 5

He Was There

And he was there,
Just sitting, watching.
His eyes were on me,
But I didn't care.
The rink was cold, quiet, still.
I could hear my skates scraping over the
            smooth ice,
And I could feel him there,
Just sitting, watching.
He was watching me,
But I didn't care.
And then they came,
Loud excited.
Maybe one hundred, maybe two.
And he was still there,

Just sitting, watching.
Some came and sat by him.
He whispered to them.
And then I could feel them all,
Just sitting, watching me.
What did he feel?
Why did he look?
Did he know I was aware?
He was there,
Just sitting, watching,
His eyes were on me,
But I didn't care.
Or did I?

Nancy, grade 8

Self-portrait

"the thirty eighth year"

the thirty eighth year
of my life,
plain as bread
round as a cake
an ordinary woman.

an ordinary woman.

i had expected to be
smaller than this,
more beautiful,
wiser in Afrikan ways,
more confident,
i had expected
more than this.

i will be forty soon.
my mother once was forty.

my mother died at forty four,
a woman of sad countenance
leaving behind a girl
awkward as a stork.
my mother was thick,
her hair was a jungle and
she was very wise
and beautiful
and sad.

i have dreamed dreams
for you mama
more than once.
i have wrapped me
in your skin
and made you live again
more than once.
i have taken the bones you hardened
and built daughters
and they blossom and promise fruit
like Afrikan trees.
i am a woman now.
an ordinary woman.
in the thirty eighth
year of my life,
surrounded by life,
a perfect picture of
blackness blessed,
i had not expected this
loneliness.

if it is western,
if it is the final
Europe in my mind,
if in the middle of my life
i am turning the final turn
into the shining dark
let me come to it whole
and holy
not afraid
not lonely
out of my mother's life
into my own.
into my own.

i had expected more than this.
i had not expected to be
an ordinary woman.

Lucille Clifton

Biographical note. Lucille Clifton was born in 1936 in Depew, New York. She now lives in Baltimore. In 1969, she won the YM-YWHA Discovery Award, and in 1980 the University of Massachusetts Juniper Prize. She is the author of four books of poetry, a memoir, and eighteen children's books.

Commentary. A woman at one of life's turning points looks back, to her own mother; looks into herself, at her mother's legacy; and looks ahead, to her own daughters, and the possibility of death. The spaces between the generations vibrate with failed hopes and somber dreams.

There's always a gap between how we see ourselves, and some idealized vision of who we might have been. Lucille Clifton arrives at her thirty-eighth year wanting to be a strong mother in her own right, yet drawing sustenance from memories of her mother's example.

But because her mother was in some way extraordinary, Lucille Clifton implies that it's not enough for her to be "ordinary." Her present fear comes from the subtle conjecturing that her mother would have been disappointed in her.

Her loneliness has the potential to work *for* her, to lead her toward the realization that she, too, is unique. A finer sense of her self will come from passing through the ordeal of measuring herself against an impossible standard.

1. Introduction. (Write the following words on the board, and, off to the side, as shown, the theme words for today's class.)

ordinary (line 5)   self-portrait

confident (line 11)   compare

countenance (line 17)

awkward (line 19)

Last time, we wrote about ourselves from the *outside*, first impressions and guesses about how we might appear to other people. Today, we are going to look *inside* ourselves, try to find the true facts, and then write about the way we really are.

First, I would like you to listen to this self-portrait in words, by Lucille Clifton, a poem called "the thirty eighth year," in which she looks at her own mother, at herself, and at her daughters. Then we will discuss the words I have written on the board.

(Mention here any of your own thoughts about the poem, biographical information, and commentary, as needed.)

2. Teacher reads poem aloud. (Then, define and discuss the words listed. It helps to ask for definitions from the class *first*. See what results. Try to keep the vocabulary in the context of the poem.)

ordinary: common, usual, normal. Nothing special or different about her.

confident: feeling sure of yourself and your abilities

countenance: the expression on a person's face

awkward: clumsy, embarrassed, not graceful, not confident (see above)

3. Children read poem aloud.

4. Questions. What do we mean by the word *compare?* (Point to word on blackboard.) When we compare, we say that something is different from, or like, something else.

Can you give me some examples *comparing* two things or even two people; or comparing a thing to a person, or a person to a thing?

What does Lucille Clifton *compare* herself to in the poem? (Wait for answers. Then read with emphasis as shown:)

> plain as *bread*
> round as *cake*
> awkward as a *stork*

Why do you think she talks about herself that way? She wants us to get a better sense of who she really is, and sometimes it isn't enough just to *describe* yourself without using more examples of what you are *like*, as a person. Instead of just saying, "I am plain, and round . . . I was awkward . . ." she compares herself to other things that are familiar to us, and gives us a fuller, clearer portrait in words of herself.

Now, let's look at the poem more closely.

How do you feel, now that you've heard me read the poem and you've read it yourselves a few times? How does the poem make you feel?

What is *her* mood in the poem?

What words in the poem tell you her mood?

What is "ordinary" about her? Do you think she thinks there is something wrong with being ordinary?

What kind of a person did she want to be by age thirty-eight?

What kind of a person was her mother?

Did she want to be more like her mother? How do you know?

Why is she lonely? What is making her feel so lonely now?

What is she afraid of?

What do you imagine will happen to her now?

5. The poetic theme. We have learned that in the same way a painter uses different-colored paints to create an image, a writer uses words to make people use their own imaginations so they can "see," in their minds, what he is trying to say.

Does anyone know what a *self-portrait* is? (Point to blackboard.) Has anyone ever been to an art museum and seen one? (Wait for replies.)

It's a picture of the artist done by himself, sometimes by looking in a mirror, sometimes by *imagining* what his own face looks like.

Why do you think an artist would want to paint his self-portrait? He is using the talent, skill, and imagination he has as an artist to show everyone the true image of himself, the way he really is.

What about a writer's idea of himself? What would a self-portrait in words have in it? You would want to show your version, your idea of who you are, rather than accepting someone else's impression.

Today we are going to describe ourselves from the *inside*, and write about the kind of people we are. Because no one knows you better than you! I will give you some suggestions about the things that could be included in the poem.

6. What we will write about. Here are some questions you might want to answer in the poem, to help make your self-portrait in words be true to life.

What makes you *unique?* What makes you (in other words) different from everyone else in the world?

What do you *do* that makes you you? What are your favorite activities, and why?

What things mean a lot to you and are very important to you?

What are your likes and dislikes?

What kinds of feelings do you have, when do you have them, and for what reasons do you feel them?

7. Children's poems from the book.

8. Reread poem, restate task. Remember to put a new sentence on a new line; skip a line between stanzas when you have a new idea, or come to a new part of your personality that you are describing. Be truthful. Be honest. You know yourself better than anyone else.

9. Writing.

10. Reading aloud in class. (Time permitting. This is another poem that could be completed at home with more elaboration possible.)

Myself

I am a girl
who likes almost anything—
tennis, languages,
and almost any sport.
I have an intention
to bè a tennis pro
known throughout the world
known throughout the world, that is,
as a person
who takes her profession seriously.

Marsha, grade 5

Me

I'm a person two in one

In the inside I have feelings,
sometimes they don't show,
but when they do they really do.

When I see hate I get very cold inside.

When I see friendship my face lights up.

Linda, grade 5

Five

When I was four,
I wished I was five.
Being five was my goal.
My most important thing.
Five came so slowly.

When I was four,
I was wishing I was five.
It seemed that
I would never be five.
Five came so slowly.

Then I was five.
Finally five.
I had to count my age
On one full hand.
Five was so nice.

Then I was six,
Already six.
It seemed just yesterday,
That I was four.
Five went so fast.
Five.

Harold, grade 8

Self as other

Walking Poem

How beautifully the child I carry on my back
teaches me to become a horse.
How quickly I learn to stay
between shafts, blinders, and whips,
bearing the plough

and the wagon loaded with hay,
or to break out of trot and run
till we're flying through cold streams.
He who kicks my commands
knows I am ten times his size

and that I am servant to small hands.
It is in mowed fields I move best,
watching the barn grow toward me,
the child quiet, his sleep piled like hay
on my back as we slip over the dark hill

and I carry the sun away.

Nancy Willard

Biographical note. Nancy Willard was born and raised in Ann Arbor, Michigan. She teaches at Vassar College and lives in Poughkeepsie, New York. She tells us, "When my son was an infant, I used to carry him in a back carrier that allowed him to see the world over my shoulders. I hope readers of 'Walking Poem' will read it as a celebration of walking, carrying, and caring for."

Commentary. The idea of transformation is endlessly attractive to the poet. In this lovely poem, a mother is inspired by her son to "change" herself into an imagined horse. She does so by an act of will, and then sustains the fantasy all the way through. She imagines that there truly is a connection among all things. Her son teaches her how to be something different, for a while. He knows what in fact he cannot know, being so young.

The entire experience grows out of that first moment when she puts him on her back. Appropriately, it ends with the child, once again a child, lulled to sleep by his mother, once again a mother.

---

1. Introduction. (Write the following words on the board and off to the side, as shown, the theme for today's class.)

shafts (line 4)	change yourself into
blinders (line 4)	another person, animal,
plough (line 5)	or thing

Last time, we wrote about our *true* selves, self-portraits in words that described the way we really are. Today, we are going to *pretend* to become someone or something else, and write about what that would be like.

First, I want to read you a poem by Nancy Willard called "Walking Poem," in which she carries her baby son on her back and imagines that she is a horse. Then we will discuss the words I have written on the board.

(Mention here any of your own thoughts on the poem, biographical information, and commentary, as needed.)

2. Teacher reads poem aloud. (Then, define and discuss the words listed. It helps to ask for definitions from the class *first*. See what results. Try to keep the children in the context of the poem. All of the words listed below have to do with the trappings of being a horse pulling a "wagon loaded with hay," so they can be discussed as a group. Make certain that the children understand how these words help complete the image of her self as a horse.)

shafts: two long, slender poles attached to the front of the wagon, leading to either side of the horse

blinders: flaps on the horse's bridle, covering his eyes, so that he cannot be distracted by objects at his sides

plough: a farming machine used to cut, lift, turn over, and sometimes grind up the soil, preparing it for planting

3. Children read poem aloud.

4. Questions. How do you feel, now that you've heard me read the poem and you've read it yourselves a few times? How does the poem make you feel?

Where does this poem take place, in the city or the country? How can you tell?

Does Nancy Willard *really* turn into a horse, or does she use her imagination to think about what it would be like if she *were* a horse?

Once she has imagined herself as a horse, what does she do?

Where does she go?

Has anyone in class ever ridden a horse?

How do you *communicate* with a horse; that is, how do you tell him what you want him to do, what direction to go, how fast to go, when to slow down? (Then read from the poem,

"He who kicks my commands
knows I am ten times his size . . .")

Why do you think she turns around and goes back at the end of the poem?

What time of day is it at the end? How do you know?

What does she mean by "I carry the sun away"?

(Write on the board, sun–son. Then read the line twice, showing the children how the two words sound alike. Perhaps the poet wants us to understand *two* different things in that line: that it is the end of day; and that she is carrying her child, her son.)

5. The poetic theme. (Some thoughts for the teacher: We've reached a point now where we want

99

the children to consider the concept of *imagined changing*. "Image" and "self" have been explored to an extent; this exercise is a synthesis of those two ideas, and then takes a further step, and explores what possibilities lie beyond the boundaries of our selves seen in realistic terms.

In the very choices the children make about who or what they would like to be, by implication they make statements about themselves as themselves. Who you remind yourself of, or who/what you *might* be, are indicators about who you actually *are*.

We never stray too far from the focus upon self-discovery and self-definition. Of course, we are human; and magic transformations such as Nancy Willard's can only occur in "the mind's eye." Sometimes, though, in the process of doing something intrinsically human as, in her case, carrying her son on her back, we find ourselves thinking about someone or something else performing the very same act.

Poetry is the most appropriate way to take on these kinds of questions, because, as we have been trying to establish, the poem accommodates all possible variations. This "transformation exercise" not only stretches the children's imaginative powers one dimension further—it stretches their awareness of what poems can do, what poems can hold.)

6. What we will write about. Imagine this. Have you ever wondered what it would be like if you could be any other person in the world?

Who would you be? What if you could become an animal? Which animal would you be? If you could change yourself into a thing, what thing would you be?

Then, once you become this person, or animal, or thing, how would you spend your time? What would you *do* all day?

Where would you go? How would you live? How would you speak, if you could speak? What would you eat?

What are the good and bad things—the advantages and disadvantages—of being this person, animal, or thing? What good things would happen to you, and what bad things?

(Point to the theme phrase on blackboard.) I'd like you to write about changing yourself into another person, animal, or thing. The questions I've asked should give you a good idea of how to go about it. Here's a good way to start. Write it as if you were that person, animal, or thing: "I am . . ." and talk to us in that way. It's easier to get your ideas down by beginning with "I."

7. Children's poems from the book.

8. Reread poem, restate task.
You see the way Nancy Willard can convince us that she is a horse: by doing the things that horses do; and her son is riding her, the way people do when they actually sit on a horse's back.

Remember to put a new sentence on a new line; skip a line between stanzas when you have a new idea, or come to a new part of your imagined self that you're describing. Don't forget, you *are* another person; you *are* another animal; you *are* another thing. Let's find out what life would be like for you!

9. **Writing.**

10. **Reading aloud in class.**

What I Am

I am the best swimmer in the world
I am a fish
I can stay underwater as long as I want
I have a lot of friends when I swim in the ocean
But the sharks always try to eat me
I make friends with the small fish
I know better than to bite on a piece of worm
When I was little
a baby trout tried to make friends with me
But I did not know that
so I went under a rock

When I got older it was harder for me
to travel through the water
Then I couldn't get anything to eat
So when a piece of worm came down
I ate it and someone caught me
So whoever you are
please don't if you are a fish,
don't bite on a piece of worm!

Good Luck!

Todd, grade 3

The Great Bald Eagle

I am an eagle
hot and thirsty
So are my friends
hot and thirsty
Catching and catching
all day long
living in the hills
and flying so high

So hot! So hot!

Chris, grade 4

Departing

The leaves,
Orange, yellow, and green,
Arrange themselves from branch to branch
Almost as if they
Had a form to follow.

The branches
seem to let go,
As if they didn't want us anymore,
We haven't done anything wrong.

The grass all shiny green
Greets us,
A soft bed it offers but
Bad things happen.
We get pushed off among
a crowd,
And I thought departing would
Be fun.

Pat, grade 8

Self to other

Duck-chasing

I spied a very small brown duck
Riding the swells of the sea
Like a rocking chair. "Little duck!"
I cried. It paddled away,
I paddled after it. When it dived,
Down I dived: too smoky was the sea,
We were lost. It surfaced
In the west. I torpedoed west
And when it dived I dived,
And we were lost and lost and lost
In the slant smoke of the sea.
When I came floating up on it
From the side, like a deadman,
And yelled suddenly, it took off,
It skimmed the swells as it ascended,
Brown wings burning and flashing
In the sun as the sea it rose over
Burned and flashed underneath it.
I did not see the little duck again.
Duck-chasing is a game like any game.
When it is over it is all over.

Galway Kinnell

Biographical note. Galway Kinnell was born in 1927, and has lived in Europe, Iran, and Hawaii. He has taught at numerous universities all over the U.S. His books of poetry include *The Book of Nightmares* (1971) and *Body Rags* (1967). He tells us, "I wrote 'Duck-chasing' while living in Nice, France. I was describing an actual game I would play with the ducks in the water. As I wrote the poem, it occurred to me it had wider application, and this realization is what produced the last few lines."

Commentary. It doesn't really matter what he might say to the duck were he to catch up with it; or what he might do. The game is all—and it begins and ends suddenly, arbitrarily.

We wonder about the futility of even attempting duck-chasing in the first place. But, as we have seen before, this is part of the poet's business—to take risks, even if a kind of failure results.

The situation has its clearly defined and delightful challenge. He applies himself to consistent pursuit and keeps going as long as possible, until, in retrospect, he learns his lesson from the situation.

It can be very important to have some real or imagined "other" when we're writing certain kinds of poems, when we want to set up a degree of urgency. Here, the single-minded pursuit, for whatever reason, of a little duck, makes for a poem with a clean sweep, a single brush stroke from start to finish.

Introduction. (Write the following words on the board, and off to the side, as shown, the theme for today's class.)

swells (line 2)   voice
torpedoed (line 8)
slant (line 11)   talking to someone
ascended (line 15)   or something else

Last time, we pretended to *become* something or someone else and wrote about what that would be like.

Today, we are going to *talk to* someone or something else, in our poems. First, I want to read you a poem by Galway Kinnell called "Duck-chasing," in which he plays a very unusual game. Then, we will discuss the words I have written on the board.

(Mention here any of your own thoughts on the poem, biographical information, and commentary, as needed.)

2. Teacher reads poem aloud. (Then, define and discuss the words listed. It helps to ask for definitions from the class *first*. See what results. Try to keep the children in the context of the poem.)

swells: waves. We think of more gently curving waves when we hear this word. Perhaps he wanted the lovely sound and rhythmic effect of "swells of the sea."

torpedoed: A torpedo is a self-propelling, submarine-like object shot from one vessel to another with the intent of damaging it. Here, of course, he is comparing his swimming actions with those of a torpedo, projecting himself rapidly under the water, no destruction intended!

slant: sloping down at an angle. Here, we think of the sunlight filtering deeply down from the surface of the water, creating shadows and obscurity.

ascended: went up. The duck takes off from the surface of the water.

3. Children read poem aloud.

4. Questions. How do you feel, now that you've heard me read the poem and you've read it yourselves a few times? How does the poem make you feel?

He says at the end that "Duck-chasing is a game." What is a game? (Ask for suggestions from class and make a list of definitions on the board; i.e., how many people to play it, rules, time limits—when it starts and ends, etc.)

How do you play the game of duck-chasing? Are there any rules?

Who would you imagine to be more at home in the sea? The man or the duck? Who would be more used to being there?

Did you notice how many times he tells us that he and the duck were "lost"? (Repeat quotes from poem.) Why do you suppose he does that?

You remember we discussed how poets *compare* themselves to things in poems. What does he compare himself to here (a torpedo, deadman), and why?

What does he *compare* the duck to at the beginning of the poem (a rocking chair), and why?

Do you think he enjoys the game of duck-chasing? How can you tell from the poem if he does or doesn't?

Do you think that he learned some kind of lesson at the end, after the duck-chasing game, that it *taught* him something? What might he have learned?

Do you think he had something particular in mind that he wanted to say to the duck?

Let's imagine for a moment that he did catch the duck, and that he could *communicate* with it, that it could *understand* him. What do you think he would say to the duck? What would the duck say to him?

5. The poetic concept and the poetic theme. How do we tell one person from another when they are speaking?

Our *voice* is the sound we make when we *express* ourselves to one another. (Point to the word on the blackboard.)

People may sound very much alike, but no two people in the world have the same voice. What can you tell about a person from his voice, from the way he expresses himself? How do we use our voices to change the meaning of what we are saying?

(Reread the poem at this point. Ask the children to listen for the voice of the poet.)

Notice that the first time he speaks to the duck he "cries." What does that mean here? Does it mean that he is crying because he is unhappy, or is it a different kind of cry?

Then, later on in the poem, he "yelled." What's

the difference between a *cry* and a *yell*? (You could risk asking a few of the children to demonstrate, if you feel the others can take it!)

He is trying to reach out to this little duck, to get his attention somehow, but what does he do instead? What happens? How does the duck react to his cries and yells?

Now, suppose we wanted to use *our* voices in writing. How could we tell a poem by one person in our class from a poem by another person? After a while, we begin to get used to the way certain people write in their own special ways.

Just as each person in this class has his or her very own way of talking to others, we also have our own ways of *writing* that are unique and special to us.

(You might want to read a few poems from one or two children and point out what you have noticed by now about the way they express themselves, if a thread of consistency can be determined. By now, there should be certain characteristics emerging in some of the children's writing which you can indicate to the others.)

Today, we are going to use our own voices in writing, and speak to someone or something else on paper, in a poem. Let me explain what I mean.

6. What we will write about. I'm sure that all of you have certain things you'd like to say to a *person* you know, or used to know, that you have never said, or have always wanted to say.

Or, maybe you have a *pet* that you wish could understand English so that you could have a conversation with it?

Or, maybe you'd even like to be able to talk to a *thing*—like your family car, or your house, or school, or a flower, or the TV set. What would you say if this thing could actually understand you?

Choose a person, or an animal, or a thing that you would really like to talk to on paper, and use your voices as if you were really talking—to say what is on your mind.

It might help to pretend that you are writing a letter to this person, animal, or thing. That might help get you started.

7. Children's poems from the book.

8. Restate task. (No need to reread the poem, as we've already done so earlier.) Remember to put a new sentence on a new line; skip a line between stanzas when you have a new idea, or come to something different that you are saying. Don't be afraid to say what you have always wanted to say, to write as if you were talking to that person, animal, or thing.

9. Writing.

10. Reading aloud in class.

You

I watch and wonder
what makes you seem as though
you are not participating
in a world that changes daily
You seem like a box of memories
shut off in a closet never changing
just gathering dust
yet a spark might ignite
and then you turn back into the world
you have been shut off from
You get peace in silence
and express yourself fully
when no-one seems to listen
A fantasy-world fills your box
of memories as you shut yourself
off again

Sara, grade 8

To my dog

Mandy, I want to say I'm sorry for every time I
kick you off the end of my bed and every time
that I hit you but you deserved it sometimes.
You're really not a bad dog and I like you a lot.
But there's one thing wrong with you. You
should stop barking when someone's there and
then run underneath the table. You know the dog

is supposed to protect man and that we're not supposed to protect you! And another thing. You shouldn't wake me up just to let you out. Go to dad. Let him let you out. I like to play with you—you act so silly, especially when we squirt orange peels at your nose.

Tracey, grade 7

To My Shoe

For 5 straight months I've worn you on my foot.
Although I have others you are the pair I've worn
    most.
You've been on my foot through good and bad.
You were there when I laughed and felt happy.
You were there when I was lonely and depressed.
You've got a lot of spunk, shoe.
You never even seemed to mind when I soaked
you in a mud puddle or threw you at the dog.
But now as my foot grows longer and wider
I see that I just can't wear you anymore.
So now all those memories of laughter and
loneliness, mud puddles and dogs,
lie in a shoe box on the top closet shelf,
while another pair of shoes are just beginning
to look dirty.

Leslie, grade 7

◆

Part IV
My Personal
World

◆

Environment

One Home

Mine was a Midwest home—you can keep your world.
Plain black hats rode the thoughts that made our code.
We sang hymns in the house; the roof was near God.

The light bulb that hung in the pantry made a
    wan light,
but we could read by it the names of preserves—
outside, the buffalo grass, and the wind in the night.

A wildcat sprang at Grandpa on the Fourth of July
when he was cutting plum bushes for fuel,
before the Indians pulled the West over the edge
    of the sky.

To anyone who looked at us we said, "My friend";
liking the cut of a thought, we could say, "Hello."
(But plain black hats rode the thoughts that made our code.)

The sun was over our town; it was like a blade.
Kicking cottonwood leaves we ran toward storms.
Wherever we looked the land would hold us up.

William Stafford

Biographical note. William Stafford was born in 1914. He now lives in Lake Oswego, Oregon, and teaches at Lewis and Clark College. He tells us, "I felt strong allegiances to our home in Kansas, to our area, to the practices and values and people around: my poem, "One Home," simply ranges through a number of the recollected scenes, rooms, stories we cherished. Writing the poem, I luxuriated in the particulars—the pantry, the hymns, the buffalo grass. And back of what actually got into the words were many other parts of our life—my mother getting jars out of the pantry, the sound of the cottonwood leaves when they blew along the streets. And through all of these particulars, I felt the thread, the abiding nearness of friends and family, with their plain ways and their faith in what surrounded them, and in what they shared with each other."

Commentary. With the calm, ordered, yet always natural precision that characterizes so much of his poetry, William Stafford subtly evokes a childhood time long past. This poem reminds us of the importance of keeping our eyes and ears open to the simple details in our daily world. This is where poetry begins, close to home, out of immediate circumstances: The things we take for granted are often the most appropriate for poetry.

"Plain black hats rode the thoughts that made our code": this line, repeated refrain-like in the poem, evokes more than any other the particulars of that time and place. It was a simple life, but not an easy one; austere, but not too solemn; spiritual, but also connected to the earth. Against the broad plains landscape, memories stand clearly etched.

---

1. Introduction. (The preceding group of four lessons concentrated upon helping the children formulate images of themselves from various perspectives. In this lesson, and the two following, we will turn our attention *outward*, to the places around us, and explore—again, from different points of view and with different emphases—our personal worlds. We will exercise our perceptions of what's supposedly familiar. In so doing, we will discover about the unfamiliar.

Write the following words on the board, and off to the side, as shown, the theme for today's class.)

code (line 2)   environment
pantry (line 4)
wan (line 4)
buffalo grass (line 6)
plum bushes (line 8)
cottonwood (line 14)

Today, I'd like to read you a poem called "One Home," by William Stafford. It's a memory full of images of his childhood in a small Kansas town. Close your eyes while I read it. You will see what he saw. Then we will discuss the words I have written on the board.

(Mention here any of your thoughts on the poem, biographical information, and commentary, as needed.)

2. Teacher reads poem aloud. (Then, define and discuss the words listed. It helps to ask for definitions from the class *first*. See what results. Try to keep the children in the context of the poem.)

code: law. Here, perhaps the unwritten rules that governed daily life in the town, principles which people lived by.

pantry: a room or closet where bread and other foods are kept; usually near the kitchen

wan: faint, dim, pale. Just enough light for him to be able to "read the names of preserves."

buffalo grass: a low-growing grass very common in areas of the West where buffalo used to feed

plum bushes: William Stafford tells us, "We called these sandhill plums. They grew all around in our part of Kansas."

cottonwood: slender, shady trees, like poplars or willows

3. Children read poem aloud.

4. Questions. How do you feel, now that you've heard me read the poem and you've read it yourselves a few times? How does the poem make you feel?

Why does he say, "you can keep your world"? Is he being unfriendly, or is he trying to show us how important his childhood home was to him?

"Plain black hats rode the thoughts that made our code." What do you see when I read that line to you? What kinds of images come into your mind?

Do you have an image in your mind of the town? Describe how you think it looks.

What kind of life do you think these people led?

What sorts of *sounds* do you hear in the poem? Are they city or country sounds? (hymns . . . wind . . . said . . . storms)

Were people friendly to each other in the town? How can you tell from the poem?

How do you think William Stafford feels now, looking back to those early days? Do you think he has happy memories of the past?

5. The poetic theme. Does anyone know what the word *environment* means? (Point to blackboard.)

Our environment is our *surroundings;* everything that surrounds us, that is all around us, wherever we might be. Our house. The street we live on. Our neighborhood. Our town. All that is *familiar* to us, that we see every day.

Let's start with your own room. How many of you could *describe* your room environment? Remember when we talked about describing something, making a word picture? How would you begin? With what part of your room? What's the most important part of your room environment? Would you describe your room as if you were standing in the doorway looking in, or sitting on your bed, or as if you were looking in through the window? (Ask for responses from the children.)

How well do you think you could describe all the things you see on your way to school every day? (Ask the class how they get to school; by what means, what route they take from their home to school, what landmarks they pass by, how carefully they look around them.)

How about this town/city/village, etc.? Do you

think you could *describe* it? Where would you begin, if you had to write a description of our town? Would you have to visit every part of it to write a good description?

A poet has to become more and more *aware,* more *awake* to the world around him—to the little things he sees and hears every day. Most of us take these things for granted. But once we begin to *notice* them, and practice noticing them, we understand how much there truly is to write about.

6. What we will write about. Today, we're going to choose some part of our environment and describe what it looks like and what happens in it.

Perhaps you'd like to write about what goes on at your house on a typical Saturday; or what makes your neighborhood unique and different; or maybe you'd just like to focus very simply upon your own room: what's in it, how you've made it reflect *you,* and the things you like to do.

Or, perhaps you'd like to describe a place you visit or go to often, like this school, or even this classroom. Or try to describe the whole town, the way William Stafford did in his poem.

I'd like you to show as much as you can about the sights, sounds, and events in the environment you choose to describe.

7. Children's poems from the book.

8. Reread poem, restate task. Remember, put a new sentence on a new line; skip a line between stanzas—the way William Stafford does (hold up the book so the children can see the precise alignment of five three-line stanzas), when you have a new idea, or come to a different part of your environment.

9. Writing.

10. Reading aloud, in class.

My Room

I walk in my orange door
and step on my green carpet
I walk over to my bed
and sit on my yellow bedspread
I turn on my stereo
with a flick of the yellow button
I pick up my yellow bean bag chair
and throw it against my green desk
My yellow bulletin board falls
and hits my orange garbage can
and the white papers go all over
and wreck the whole scene

Paula, grade 8

My Neighborhood

My street is very noisy.
There's so much noise and crimes
happening on our street.

It is a very bad place to live
for younger people who are growing
older.

There's so much filth and dirt
surrounding us
that we're going to move
to a piece of land that we bought.

There's this lady who lives
across the street who is very nosy.
Every night she always has to peek
through her window to see
what we're doing.

But what do you expect for a
lady who is all alone and doesn't
have anything to do.

Miriam, grade 5

In the house
Children fighting
Dogs barking

Outside—bright, cool, quiet.
On the pond—laughter, someone falls,
Ice skates click.

In the fields—a cat drags home her prize,
The snow is gently falling, now.

In a tree—a squirrel gnaws on a nut.

Marie, grade 7

Favorite place

The Ideal Retreat

I will choose a place where the snakes feel safe.
All day I will love that remote country.
At times I will climb the peak of its lonely
    mountain
to stay and whistle until the sky grows cold.

W.S. Merwin
translation of poem by Khong Lo

Biographical note. W.S. Merwin was born in 1927 in New York City, and grew up in New Jersey and Pennsylvania. Since the 1950s he has made much of his living through translation. He writes, "I began translating with the idea that it could teach me something about writing poetry . . . Ezra Pound spoke of the value of translation as a means of continually sharpening a writer's awareness of the possibilities of his own language."

Commentary. This is a poem of essentials; spare, graceful, declarative. It points toward a wished-for situation in a far-off place, where the poet can be removed from all the trappings of his everyday world.

It's important to notice how he *personalizes* the *place*, imposes his own needs and requirements upon it. We all have different reasons for desiring this kind of isolation, whether it be internal or actual. We can move to a "remote country" within the landscape of our own minds, as well as some outer geography.

Because it is so brief, the poem is extremely evocative, forcing us to come back again and again. Its purely conditional aspect is tantalizing. The poem must be stated as a future possibility: "I will." We may conclude by wondering what prevents him from closing the gap between real and ideal. And that opens up another realm of possibilities.

---

1. Introduction. (This lesson takes the generalized environment one step further into focus. We ask the children to take a look at a particular aspect of their real or imagined/idealized environments, and to write about why that place is their favorite place. We go beyond the actuality of description to the process of evaluation.

Write the following words on the board, and off to the side, as shown, the theme for today's class.)

ideal (title)
retreat (title)   your favorite place
remote (line 2)
peak (line 3)

This is another very short poem that manages to say a great deal in just four lines. Last time, we talked and wrote about our environments. Today, I'd like to read you a poem translated into English from Vietnamese by W.S. Merwin. It is called "The Ideal Retreat." It is about a man who wants to get away from it all, away from the cares and troubles of his everyday life. After I read it to you, and we discuss the words I've written on the board, and ask some questions, we will write about *our* favorite places.

(Mention here any additional thoughts on the poem, biographical information, and commentary, as needed.)

2. Teacher reads poem aloud. (Then, define and discuss the words listed. It helps to ask for definitions from the class *first*. See what results. Try to keep the children in the context of the poem.)

ideal: existing in the imagination (which we've discussed at length previous to this lesson); perfect *retreat:* a place of privacy, seclusion, and safety; also, a *hiding* place (this is important for later discussion)

remote: distant, out of the way, separate

peak: the highest point of a mountain

3. Children read poem aloud.

4. Questions. How do you feel, now that you've heard me read the poem and you've read it yourselves a few times? How does the poem make you feel?

Let's look more closely at the poem, one line at a time. (Hold the book up to the children once again, so that the true brevity of this poem is made evident.)

Do snakes like people?

What kind of place do snakes like? What kind of place would make them "feel safe"?

Has he ever actually gone to this place? How can you tell from the poem whether or not he has actually *been* there?

What would he do if he got to this place?

Why do you imagine he wants to go there?

Why do you think he has not gone there yet?

What is stopping him from going there? Do you think perhaps he is a little afraid?

Does this sound like the kind of place that you would like to visit?

Well, then, what would *your* "ideal retreat" — favorite place — look like? (Leads into discussion that follows.)

5. Poetic theme and 6. What we will write about. (The poem is succinct and direct. We don't want to belabor it.

The purpose of the discussion is to guide the children toward an awareness of personalized places, either imagined or real, which they have made their own.

Part of that process is the repeated act of going there and being there; or, if it is a fantasy place, of thinking about it and creating images of it.

We have asked in previous lessons, "What do you do that makes you, you?" Now we want to know what it is about these places that makes them favorite.)

The poet in "The Ideal Retreat" wants to find a "remote country," to be alone, to achieve solitude, to have peace and quiet, a change from his usual life.

Do any of you have a secret place, a hideaway, where no one can find you? Or, perhaps a place where you go to meet your friends, a place where you all come together? (If the children are willing, ask them to give some examples of hiding places and places where they congregate. Even their reluctance to divulge this kind of personal, special information can help you remind them that these places are unique, for whatever reasons.)

Once you are at these hiding places or gathering places, what do you do there? If these are imaginary places, what *would* you do there?

I'd like each of you to choose: a place you go to hide, to get away from everyone; or a place you go with your family (for example, on vacation); or a place you imagine you would really like to be.

Then, I'd like you to tell me in a poem where this place is; why it is a favorite for you; what you do when you are there; why you need to go there, or wish you could go there.

This favorite place can be real or made up.

7. Children's poems from the book.

8. Reread poem, restate task. Remember, put a new sentence on a new line; skip a line between stanzas when you have a new idea, or come to a different aspect of your favorite place.

We want to know why this is a favorite place, and what you do there.

9. Writing.

10. Reading aloud in class.

My Perfect Place

My perfect place
has rainbows every day
with bright pinks, greens,
blues, and yellows.

My perfect place
has a warm, yellow sun
in the day
and a light rain every night.

My perfect place
has tulips, roses,
lilacs, and marigolds
in bright reds, yellows,
oranges, and pinks.

My perfect place
has many people
with everyone smiling
and being friends.

My perfect place
has a beautiful house.
That is where I live.

My perfect place
has many animals,
all friends.

Maria, grade 4

My favorite place is in my bedroom.
I have my dolls there.
I am glad that I have someone to talk to.
My dolls listen to me.
No one else will listen to me like they do.

Lisa, grade 4

Squatting by a pond
Grass and weeds standing about me taller than I
    was,
Ready to pounce at the
first frog in sight.
Quietly not
speaking hardly breathing.
Being there for hours
on hours just waiting
to cup my hands on
a frog.

  Small and green.
  Very quick.

Kristen, grade 9

There's the smell of pine trees often
Problems and cares go away
Just wish it, it'll happen
to me, to you
Wish a soda
Wish a steak
It can happen
If you want it you can get it
so wish

Where am I?
Paradise

Brian, grade 6

Usual/unusual

Snowfall in the Afternoon

I.

The grass is half-covered with snow.
It was the sort of snowfall that starts in the late
    afternoon,
And now the little houses of the grass are
    growing dark.

II.

If I reached my hands down, near the earth,
I could take handfuls of darkness!
A darkness was always there, which we never
    noticed.

III.

As the snow grows heavier, the cornstalks fade
    farther away,
And the barn moves nearer to the house.
The barn moves all alone in the growing storm.

IV.

The barn is full of corn, and moving toward us
    now,
Like a hulk blown toward us in a storm at sea;
All the sailors on deck have been blind for many
    years.

Robert Bly

Biographical note. Robert Bly was born in 1926, in Madison, Minnesota. He tells us, "When I wrote "Snowfall in the Afternoon" we had recently moved to the farm, after having lived in New York City for several years. We had no lawnmower, so the grass on the front lawn grew quite long by fall. The first snow came in early November, and this is a poem that came while watching the snow fall that day in its deliciousness.

"The long grass turned out to be a blessing, because, bending over, it made small houses as the snow weighed it down. I got very interested in those houses.

"Looking up, I noticed the cornstalks still in the field seemed farther away—that was just an optical illusion. The barn, oddly, did not have hay that year, but kernel corn 'sealed' under a government price-support program, so it was sort of a treasure holder. But as I looked at it, I got the opposite impression. I saw a sort of ghost ship, blown before the wind; on the decks I saw sailors, thin, and in rags, with eyes frozen shut—by the sleet perhaps. The image surprised me when it came, so much so that I ended the poem right there.

"Sometimes, a poem carries a message from the writer over to those who hear it; at other times, the poem carries some message to the writer himself. In this case, the last line saddened me for days, and made me thoughtful on the point for months, since it said clearly that I was blind, and had been for some time."

Commentary. Two different strains play against each other in this mysterious poem: on the one

133

hand, simple diction and an immediately noticeable structure (four numbered three-line stanzas); on the other, an atmosphere of surreal images. The final effect is definitive, moving, and powerful.

Notice how Bly transforms a simple scene by looking so deeply at what he sees. His gaze outward over the snowy fields becomes a trance.

Poetry sometimes comes into being through this kind of heightened concentration.

---

1. Introduction. (The marvellous simplicity of language in this poem welcomes us. The basic conversational tone leads subtly and surely into a mysterious realm of strange images and ominous impressions. Children enjoy its pleasant yet ghostly quality. This lesson concentrates upon the interplay of *usual* language with *unusual* image—and we ask the children to write about a similar juxtaposition, drawing once again upon their own experiences.

Write the following word on the board—this is the only one in the poem that should be difficult— and off to the side, as shown, the theme for today's class.)

hulk (line 11)   usual

unusual

Today's poem is called "Snowfall in the Afternoon" by Robert Bly. It has some very strange images. While I am reading the poem to you, I'd like you to listen very closely for the unusual pictures he creates, so that we can talk about them later. After we read and discuss it, we will try to write about something strange from our own lives.

(Mention here any additional thoughts on the poem, biographical information, and commentary, as needed.)

2. Teacher reads poem aloud. (Then, define and discuss the word below. It helps to ask for definitions from the class *first*. See what results. Try to keep the children in the context of the poem.)

hulk: a heavy, clumsy ship (He *compares* the barn to a hulk. Review back to this concept: the idea that we can bring together two different things in a poem, to help make our images more effective and different.)

3. Children read poem aloud.

4. Questions. How do you feel, now that you've heard me read the poem and you've read it yourselves a few times? How does the poem make you feel?

(Hold up the book and show the poem to the class so that they can see how Bly has divided it into four clearly numbered stanzas.)

In the other poems we have read, have the stanzas been numbered like this? Why do you suppose Robert Bly decided to number each stanza? What is he trying to make us *notice* about the poem? Let's look at each stanza separately, and pretend that each one is a separate poem by itself. Each stanza seems to have something strange and unusual about it.

(Read each stanza aloud, pausing to discuss the images in each, as listed below.)

I. "the little houses of the grass"—What are they? Who or what do you imagine would live in these houses?

135

II. "handfuls of darkness"—How do you pick up darkness? What might this darkness be? Why is it that "we never noticed" it before?

III. "the barn moves nearer to the house"—If you don't believe that the barn is *really* moving, what do you suppose he is telling us there? Have *you* ever tried to look at something in the distance through a swirling snowstorm?

IV. "the barn . . . like a hulk"—What is the very strange thing that has happened in this stanza? He's really using his imagination now, isn't he? Who is on this imaginary ship in the middle of the snowstorm? What are they doing there?

He uses a lot of *seeing* words in the poem. He shows us what he sees during the storm. Does he use any *hearing* words? Why not?

What is the main sound you would expect to hear during a snowstorm in the middle of the prairies?

What do you think his *mood* is at the end of the poem? Compare it to the way he feels at the beginning. What happened?

5. The poetic theme. (In building gradually upon the concept of image—now through another environmental approach—we're trying to move the children toward an awareness of seeing more in what's already there. "Snowfall in the Afternoon" takes a very commonplace situation, and makes it unusual.

Point to the theme words on the blackboard. Again, ask for definitions from the class.)

    usual: ordinary, familiar
    unusual: rare, strange, different

Robert Bly shows us some unusual things happening during a usual situation in his life. What about you? Can anyone here give an example of something that happened, beginning in a usual way, and ending in an unusual way? Something that took you by surprise?

Let's make a list on the board of some of these things. (Draw a line down the center of the blackboard. Make the heading for the left side, USUAL; the heading for the right side, UNUSUAL. Ask for contributions from the children. As the list grows, they will see the contrast between the two ideas.)

6. What we will write about. Everything doesn't always happen the way we expect it to. And sometimes, very familiar things we do can seem strange, if we think about them long enough! Today, we are going to pick something that happened to us that began in the usual, familiar, ordinary way—and ended in an unusual, strange, different way. Now's your chance to try to write a "surprise ending," or to take a look at the things you do and see which you take for granted, and show us how unusual they are.

7. Children's poems from the book. (Both these examples can be used as the basis for brief discussion. You might ask what is being made to seem unusual; and in Lisa's poem, just what is actually happening to her? Notice how she uses the repetition of phrases to create an eerie effect. Joe *compares* the usual things in his neighborhood to unusual phenomena.)

8. Reread poem (unless you feel you have gone over it enough with the children during the question period), **restate task.** Remember, put a new sentence on a new line; skip a line between stanzas when you have a new idea, or come to something more unusual. Remember that the more usual your beginning, the more unusual your ending will seem to be.

9. Writing.

10. Reading aloud in class. (Time permitting. This lesson may run over.)

Driving through busy streets
All strangers.
Turning turning.
Dizzy all over.
Came to a gate
Barriers lifting to and fro.

Driving through busy parking lots
All strangers.
Turning turning.
Dizzy all over.
We are here
We are at the big building.

Walking through busy halls
All strangers.
Turning turning.
Dizzy all over.
I am here
Now alone in a room.

Everything's changed now
I am not scared
My parents are with me
Dizzy all over
Soon in a hospital bed
A plastic tent with a zipper

Lisa, grade 5

My Neighborhood

Our block is a maze
winding streets turning around
Each side of the street is a mirror image
Reflecting one side from another
Asphalt driveways burning melting like a tar pit
waiting for its catch
People are like mannequins jumping
and walking freely and wildly, always alive
Putt! Putt! Cars going down the street
Making little noise
Houses are blocks
like that of a child
who has put them in neat rows
spacing them neatly.

Joe, grade 5

The Last Words of
My English Grandmother
1920

There were some dirty plates
and a glass of milk
beside her on a small table
near the rank, disheveled bed—

Wrinkled and nearly blind
she lay and snored
rousing with anger in her tones
to cry for food,

Gimme something to eat—
They're starving me—
I'm all right I won't go
to the hospital. No, no, no

Give me something to eat
Let me take you
to the hospital, I said
and after you are well

you can do as you please.
She smiled, Yes
you do what you please first
then I can do what I please—

Oh, oh, oh! she cried
as the ambulance men lifted
her to the stretcher—
Is this what you call

making me comfortable?
By now her mind was clear—
Oh you think you're smart
you young people,

she said, but I'll tell you
you don't know anything.
Then we started.
On the way

we passed a long row
of elms. She looked at them
awhile out of
the ambulance window and said,

What are all those
fuzzy-looking things out there?
Trees? Well I'm tired
of them and rolled her head away.

William Carlos Williams

Biographical note. William Carlos Williams was born in Rutherford, New Jersey, in 1883. Aside from several early forays to Europe — and unlike most of his contemporaries, who stayed there — he spent his entire life in on small town, combining two careers with relentless energy. He wrote dozens of books: poetry, novels, short stories, essays, and the long poem *Paterson*. He was a family doctor, delivering thousands of babies and attending to the various illnesses of his townspeople for forty years.

His first book of poems, *The Tempers*, was published in 1913; many other books followed, among them: *In the American Grain* (essays, 1925), *Collected Poems* (1931), *White Mule* (a novel, 1937), *Autobiography* (1951), *Paterson* (1946-1951), and *Pictures from Breughel* (poems, 1962).

Williams's major goals as a writer were to carry forward Whitman's initiative (which we've discussed earlier); to free American verse from a rigid form inherited from England; and to do justice to a truly "American idiom" in poetry that was more natural, but still lyrical.

He died in Rutherford in 1963, and was posthumously awarded the Pulitzer Prize for Poetry.

Commentary. Hart Crane, whose poem begins this book, took a reverential view of his grandmother, acknowledging her influence upon him, yet maintaining his distance. Conversely, William Carlos Williams, whose poetry takes on the most fundamental details of life and glorifies them, sees his grandmother as contentious and engaging, right to the bitter end of her life.

The poem takes us immediately into the debris of the sick room, then moves in gradual stages outward. Notice how he sets the scene with seeming casualness; but his narrative progression is orderly and deliberate, and therefore the poem moves us by the sheer accumulation of event following upon event.

We know this is their last conversation. Something tells us it is consistent with their entire past relationship, a struggle of wills across generations: his desire and need to do his duty (after all, he was a doctor as well as a poet!) against her headstrong instinct that she is right to resist.

She manages, even when "giving up," to make one last critique of the ambiguous world. Through it all, Williams maintains a characteristically positive voice. The poet is fully aware that his poem will be the *truly* last word.

---

1. Introduction. (We conclude by shifting now from the environment of things and phenomena to the environment of persons: family and friends. However, our purpose remains the same: to take what is familiar to us and keep track of it, to *document what happens* in our lives.

Williams's poem is appealing because he's showing us the death of someone he loved, in an affirmative way. Touches here and there of wistful humor and biting wit take the somberness out of the occasion.

to the side, as shown, the theme for today's class.)
rank (line 4)   family events
disheveled (line 4)
rousing (line 7)

The poem I am about to read to you is called "The Last Words of My English Grandmother," by William Carlos Williams. You might think that a poem about death should be sad. Listen closely to this one. It might change your mind. It tells of the final conversation between the poet and his grandmother. After we read and discuss it, we'll try to write about different kinds of events in our own families.

(Mention here any additional thoughts on the poem, biographical information, and commentary, as needed.)

2. Teacher reads poem aloud. (Then, define and discuss the words listed. It helps to ask for definitions from the class *first*. See what results. Try to keep the children in the context of the poem.)

rank: foul-smelling. This is a sick room; she has been there a long time.

disheveled: disorderly, wrinkled. She's probably done a lot of tossing and turning and been quite restless.

rousing: awakening suddenly from sleep

3. Children read poem aloud. (Because of the length of the poem, it's probably best to choose just two children to read this time.)

4. Questions. How do you feel, now that you've heard me read the poem and you've read it your-

144

selves a few times? How does the poem make you feel?

Where is his grandmother? Is she in her own home? Is she happy where she is?

What does he want her to do, and what does *she* want to do?

What kind of relationship does he seem to have with his grandmother?

Do they get along well? How can you tell from the poem?

What is his grandmother's opinion about the "younger generation"? (Parenthetically, Williams was 37 years old when he wrote this.)

What does she see on her way to the hospital?

What do you think she means when she says, after seeing the trees, "I'm tired of them"? Do you think she is talking only about trees there?

How do you think Williams feels, knowing that his grandmother is going to die?

5. **The poetic theme.** (As we have demonstrated all along, poems grow most successfully from occasions that we want to keep with us. The poem has the capacity to take on extreme events such as this one: his grandmother is dying. As teachers concerned with bringing poetry to our students, we need not fear discussing death in class. Tying it to poetry is a natural and certainly acceptable way to bring up what can be a touchy, but necessary, subject. Some of the children may be too young to have experienced the loss of a close relative; which is why, in describing the task, we broaden the writing possibilities to include family events in general.

Auden said of Yeats, "Ireland hurt him into poetry." In much the same fashion, certain things that happen hurt us — either through trauma or joy or simply because they are definitive — toward expressing ourselves. In that spirit, we can talk about death with our students. We can show them that any event in their lives worth remembering is therefore worth writing about.)

Has anyone in class had a close relative who died? What did you feel at the time? I'm sure that you were sad. But what about the good things that person left behind, the things they said and did that you'll always remember? (You will, of course, want to pause here for discussion with those children willing to share memories.)

Other kinds of events besides death seem to bring families together. What would some of those be? Let's make a list on the board. (We're looking for: birth of a child, birthdays, weddings, holidays, anniversaries, graduations, etc.) These are special kinds of days that families celebrate. Do *all* of you always have fun on these days? Do *all* of you enjoy having to dress up and behave in a certain way?

(At this point it should be possible to call on people with less-than-positive opinions about these occasions, which we recall for a variety of reasons.)

6. What we will write about. Today we are going to have a *choice* of writing ideas, because I know that some of you may not wish to share the sadder times you've had; and others will not mind doing so.

Perhaps there is someone in your family, or who was very close to you, who died. Write about what happened at that time. How did the death of this person affect you? And how do you feel about it now, looking back to it? What things do you notice about this person, now that he or she is gone, that you did not see when he or she was here?

(Second choice:) Pick a family event, like the ones we've written on the blackboard. Something must have happened at one of those events that you've never forgotten. Something embarassing, or funny, or sad, or strange. Something you did, something another person said. What was enjoyable about the event? What was annoying about it?

7. Children's poems from the book. (Again, these examples have been chosen carefully to help your students understand what possibilities are open to them. They relate back directly to the description of what to write about.)

8. Restate task. Remember, put a new sentence on a new line; skip a line between stanzas when you have a new idea. I want to know, whichever you choose to write about, what remains in your mind about the person, or the family event, that you will remember for a long time to come.

9. Writing.

10. Reading aloud in class.

My Great Grandmother

We would drive up
to the big white farmhouse
on the green hill
all covered with squawking chickens
Grandma would come out
to meet us
not running
just bustling
her skin dark from long hours
in the sun
tending her garden
We would visit until
she said things
so senile even she knew
Then she would say
"Let me get you
lettuce from the garden"
and would walk to
the garden
carrying a basket
        scissors
            and 80-odd years
on her stooped back
Finally we would leave her
Then one day she
            died
and when we visited all
            we saw

was a garden
overgrown with weeds
the once neat aisles
covered with wild
                vegetables
And we realized she
                was gone

Brenda, grade 8

The Funeral

It is hot I am frightened
My mother is crying, should I?
Everyone is sad, I'm sad
Is my father crying too?

I wish I was home, I don't like this
place
Rick, my brother, is sleeping,
I can see him now
He is quiet and still, he isn't
crying should I?

Kathryn, grade 6

My fantasy: the wedding

When I was in a wedding
the flower girl asked me
to dance with her.
She said I was cute.
I ran and hid so she couldn't
find me
but she did
so I danced with her
so she wouldn't feel bad.

Oh.
I was the ring bearer.

David, grade 4

Friends

Taking Leave of a Friend

Blue mountains to the north of the walls,
White river winding about them;
Here we must make separation
And go out through a thousand miles of dead
    grass.

Mind like a floating wide cloud,
Sunset like the parting of old acquaintances
Who bow over their clasped hands at a distance.
Our horses neigh to each other
    as we are departing.

Ezra Pound
translated from Li T'ai Po

Biographical note. Ezra Pound's immeasurable influence on modern British and American writing continues full-fledged today and is virtually impossible to summarize.

He was born in Hailey, Idaho, in 1885, and attended the University of Pennsylvania. Soon after, he left for England and Italy. He spent most of his life abroad, in self-imposed exile from the United States.

Pound's literary career can be broadly divided into three phases: the first was his "Decadent" ten years in England, during which he refined his imagist approach in such books as *A Lume Spento* and *Personae*. The second period produced the Chinese translations and Noh plays, the first ten *Cantos*, *Ripostes*, and *Lustra*. Finally, he turned his entire attention to the *Cantos*, his epic work, which remained incomplete at the time of his death in 1972.

Commentary. Pound was able to respect the original languages of the poems he translated, while accommodating his own strong sense of poetics. This poem is one of the finest demonstrations I've ever seen of the way images convey emotions. It is made almost completely of images. Each one is integral and "right" when it comes. Taken together they combine to be poignant, melancholy, and uplifting.

How delicately he shapes the overwhelming Oriental landscape and the two fragile figures within it, bringing our attention down to them as they stand, poised to separate, on the edge of a vast prairie!

He sets up a lovely contrast between the undeniable presence of land and water, and the vague premonitions in the narrator's mind. We are told nothing about the actual situations, that went into the evolution of their friendship, or about why they must leave each other at this specific time. Yet we know that their drawing apart is final.

---

1. Introduction. (We have attended to the importance of family matters. Our final poetic exercise therefore addresses the issue of *friendship*: how two people become friends, what makes them stay that way, and most difficult of all, why and how they may end their friendship. Pound's poem provides us with a strong introduction to this subject of great interest to children, and also provides a fitting conclusion for our poetry lessons.

Write the following words on the board, and off to the side, as shown, the theme for today's class.)

separation (line 3)	friendship
acquaintances (line 6)	
departing (line 9)	

I'm going to read to you a translation from the Chinese. It is a short poem called, "Taking Leave of a Friend" by Ezra Pound. It's about two men who are moving away from each other. One of them is trying to express what it feels like. After we hear the poem, we'll discuss what friendship is all about and write poems about our own experiences with friends. But first, close your eyes and listen well. This poem is full of beautiful images.

(Mention here any additional thoughts on the poem, biographical information, and commentary, as needed.)

2. Teacher reads poem aloud. (Then, define and discuss the words listed. It helps to ask for definitions from the class *first*. See what results. Try to keep the children in the context of the poem.)

separation: growing apart from someone, moving away, withdrawing

acquaintances: people who know each other personally (in this case, for a long time)

departing: going away, leaving (We think of separating as coming first, a kind of prelude to departure.)

3. Children read poem aloud.

4. Questions. How do you feel, now that you've heard me read the poem and you've read it yourselves a few times? How does the poem make you feel?

You remember when we discussed *images*? (Review and redefine if necessary.) There are many images in the poem. What's the first one that comes to your mind right now?

Why are the mountains blue? And the rivers white?

"And go out through a thousand miles of dead grass"—What do you *see* when I read that line?

He *compares* two things in the poem. You remember we discussed what it means to compare? (Review and redefine if necessary.)

Who can tell me what is *compared* in the poem?

Have these two been friends for a long time? How can you tell?

Does he tell you why these two are friends? Does it really matter if you don't know why?

Does he tell you why they must separate? Does it really matter if you don't know why?

Does he use *rhyme* in the poem? Which words rhyme? (Don't forget "mind . . . wide" and "are . . . departing" as well as "acquaintance . . . distance"—that is, internal rhyme *and* end rhyme.)

Do you think these two friends will ever see each other again?

5. The poetic theme. (No preliminaries needed here; start right in with the discussion, as it will most likely be a long one.)

Let's talk about *friendship* for awhile.

How many of you have a best friend?

What *is* a friend, anyway? How is a friendship different from other kinds of relationships with people?

What do you look for in a friend? What kind of personality should he or she have?

How does a person get to be your friend? How do friendships start? Are they always planned, or do they sometimes "just happen"?

Does a person have to be *just like you* in order to be your friend, to like the same things as you; or can your friend be different from you?

How long are people usually friends? Is there a time limit on friendship?

Does your friend have to live in the same town

as you do? Do you have to see each other every day? Or can a friend be far away?

What kinds of things should friends *do* for each other?

Now: how many of you have had the experience of being friends with someone, and then *not* being friends?

How many of you have lost a friend? What kinds of things can happen to split friends up?

Can other people cause you to split up with a friend?

Can friends get back together after they stop being friends, or do you think that once someone stops being your friend, that's it forever?

6. What we will write about. Today, again, we will have two choices, both on the subject of friendship. First, you might want to do your own version, "Taking Leave of *My* Friend." This poem would be about an experience you had where a friendship ended. You would write about the kind of friendship you had, how it began, the kinds of things you and your friend did together; and then what happened to cause you to *separate* from your friend.

The other choice would be a "Portrait of My Friend." Choose one of your friends. It could be your best friend, but not necessarily. *Describe* him or her, paint a portrait of your friend in words. You remember when we did *self*-portraits; now you're going to do one of your friend. This would have to include everything about this person that makes him or her your friend.

7. Children's poems from the book.

8. Reread poem, restate task. Remember, put a new sentence on a new line; skip a line between stanzas when you have a new idea, or come to a new part of your friend that you are describing. Whichever idea you choose to write about, we need to know *why*: why you and your friend split up; *why* the person you choose is your friend.

9. Writing.

10. Reading aloud in class.

Separation

You have much fun together,
You play in the fields.
and then comes dinner time
and you go your own ways.
As you're waving and waving
good-bye you're fading away.

Kelly, grade 4

Maria

Once I had a Spanish friend
She was always laughing
Then she smiled no more
and ran into her house
I called her house
She could not speak
So I left her alone

The next day
I went out to play
Her mother stood at the door
She said, "We're moving"
Maria came to the door and said
"Gracias señorita"
And I saw her no more

Michelle, grade 4

For the friend

My friend with whom I feel quite close,
I need you here to help me.
My problems now are deep indeed,
Your consolence, dear, is sweet.

Things are different here today,
Far from things I know.
If you can help me, please do soon,
I need your help and care.

Tell me if you can come to me,
Your love I would cherish so.
And now I end my message, friend,
It helps me to let things show.

Sue, grade 9

The Girl in Locker 404

We weren't best friends
nor were we strangers
I knew her only as
the girl in locker 404

I saw her twice a day
in the morning and at two
I took for granted that
friendly smile, and occasional
How are you?

We were always the first to come
and the last to leave
I said very little to her
and she said very little to me

This went on for two months
nothing really special
Then yesterday, for the first time
I missed that smile
I don't see her anymore,
she's just not there

There's a new girl
in locker 404;
She doesn't smile
nor come home early and go home
late;
She's not like the other,
She's just the girl
in locker 404.

Joan, grade 9

CONCLUSION
◆
The Problem of Evaluation

"It will be a sad day for all of us when we teach only those things for which there are easily discernible behavioral outcomes."

—Charles Postman
Teaching as a Conserving Activity

"How can we get other persons to do and think things that count for them, for us, and for others?"

—Ken Macrorie
The Vulnerable Teacher

As a classroom teacher, you are constantly being asked to judge the performance of students. But how do you *measure* imaginative writing? How do you place a value on poetry?

To begin with, we have accepted the act of writing itself as inherently good. We are pleased that our students are putting pen to paper, and that something comes of it. We must then recognize that *no* poem which is thrust before us by an eager child can ever be called "bad," flatly and unequivocally — even if we don't like it or understand it. The wrong word from a teacher when a child is just beginning to become involved with poetry can cause irreparable damage. Poetry writing is replete with insecurity, even for the so-called professional poet.

By eliminating the possibility of labelling a child's poem as "bad," we open up to new standards by which it should be perceived. Suppose the child has heard you state the assignment for the day clearly, and several times over; and then has gone on to write something of his or her own design, has taken further initiative and spun off from what the rest of the children are doing. Perhaps in certain subjects this would be considered "wrong"; but in poetry, we'll have to remain open to it being a very positive step!

Certain *qualities* can be named, attributes to look for: inventiveness (assimilating what's been asked, then going beyond); synthesis of ideas (Does the child show an inclination to bring several ideas or images together in refreshing juxtaposition? This is the elusive technique of making *metaphors* which children seem to come by naturally.); clarity (Can you see what's being described? We've stressed this repeatedly throughout the lessons. It means that if you're going to be in a position to evaluate clarity, your own perceptions need to be honed.); music (Rhyme has been down-played throughout this book — *but* only in its unnatural states. We're encouraging and looking for sounds as they occur in the natural way.)

Strength of image is the core around which the good poem is built. By working toward word pictures, the children pull other skills along. The images carry the poem, and one sure test of the poem's success is its visual impact.

How well does the poem adhere to a *structure?* If we think of the form of a poem as its *organization,* we can evaluate how well the ideas presented move, through narrative, from beginning to end.

I must emphasize that all of these proposed standards, signs to look for and take note of, do *not* place weight upon choice of subject. The *way* in which something is said is our main concern. We will not evaluate a child's interest in one thing over another, because we're trying to broaden the scope of poetry.

Pick out an element of the poem that appears central to you on first reading, or important to the child: a line, a phrase. Pick it out, strangely enough, because it is successful *or* unsuccessful! Point to it, literally, on the paper: "That's my favorite line," or, "That's the best part of this poem," or "That's the one part of the poem that I have trouble with," or "I was with you up to that point, and then you lost me," or "What were you trying to say here?" or "I can't *see* that picture."

Zero in on a focal point. Bring it forcibly to the child's attention. Then immediately, *push* beyond it and ask for *more*.

What does this accomplish? It is the most constructive kind of evaluation you can hope to make. You are taking something from the poem and automatically using it as a jumping-off place for more writing. After a while, you'll find it impossible to accept a first draft. There will always be something to build upon, some extra margin of writing still possible.

By achieving this focus, you are showing the child that the poem has engaged you or interested you enough to make contact. After that's been demonstrated, the next step is up to him, and you're encouraging him to move on.

We see that there are indeed specific, imagination-based qualities that, with practice, we can discern in the poems presented to us. Whether they are "in" the poem or not, we take note of them, and move the child forward, even if only one more

163

word or one more line, or an erased word or line results.

This step leads very readily to *self*-editing, self-evaluation. As the teacher, your opinion is requested. You reply, "Well, what do *you* think is the best part of the poem," or, "What do *you* think is the weakest part of the poem," or, "Do you really think that's the best possible ending?"

And self-evaluation, growing from the child's sense that you have taken the time and used your attention to see his poem individually, leads once again to the discrimination needed to make poems ready for publication. This in itself is a kind of evaluation, which we'll discuss shortly.

Peer evaluation is an important part of the class process, but one which should be tried with caution. There are two ways to do it. You might like to type up a few of the poems onto stencils or dittos and distribute copies to the class, using a poem written in class as the basis for discussion. Of course, you'll want to get the author's permission first. With older children who have been writing for some time, you might want to circulate manuscripts, say, four or five poems by one person, with a cover sheet attached for people to write comments on. At any given time, there could be several manuscripts circulating in the class. This approach sometimes makes it easier for fellow students to comment, without the face-to-face requirement that embarrasses some of them.

Poems move us for intangible reasons. The classroom is usually not seen as a place where everything that happens can be objectively assessed. Poetry circumvents this assumption, replacing it with considerations of *quality*. But quality can be perceived, and the more you encourage your students to write, the more qualities will become manifest. The problem of evaluation, like the problem of writing, is best met by more opportunities for evaluation.

Practical Matters: a checklist

1. Folders: Before the poetry unit/poetry lessons begin, ask each child to make a folder (the younger children enjoy decorating them and personalizing them) into which *only poems* will go. Emphasize that this is where they should keep the work — all work related to the lessons: handouts, manuscripts, first drafts, clippings, etc. Their poems are important and should be saved, kept in one place. You can collect the folders periodically to obtain a good overview of where everyone is at any given time during the lessons.

2. Notebooks: We want to emphasize that the study of poetry goes beyond the forty minutes a day that we might be spending in class. What if you get a great idea on the bus going home, or over the weekend, or when you wake up in the morning? Small, spiral-bound notebooks, pocket-sized, are ideal for this purpose. Encourage each child to buy one (or perhaps you can convince the school to buy them for you!) and keep it handy for those surprise moments outside class. Even if nothing ever gets into them, their very existence helps expand the locales for poetry.

3. Seating plan: Row upon row of seats all facing front are fine for tests, but defeating to poetry. The best arrangement is one which allows you free and quick circulation among the children as they are writing, should they have a question, or should you want to look over their shoulders. Groups of six or so, desks pushed together, works best, especially with the younger children. Much energy is exchanged, and the children help each other and show each other works in progress. Older students, seventh-grade and up, may be less inclined to like this intimate approach.

4. Time: The lessons are planned to fit into the usual periods that mark a typical school day. However, I cannot emphasize strongly enough the importance of allowing a class to run over, of taking great care not to force each lesson into a mold. Some lessons *take* better than others. The most common occurrence will probably be that the discussion period will extend into writing time, so you'll discover the class ready to write, with five minutes left to class. Ask them to take their thoughts home, to jot down some basic ideas, to tack them up on the wall over their desks at home — anything to keep the thread of the discussion alive. Then, first thing the next day you can pick up where you left off.

Better to allow for an extension of an idea than to cut it off prematurely. As we've said previously, the *process* of getting to the point of writing is just as important as the writing itself!

5. Scheduling: There are fifteen lessons here. How shall you pace them? My own experience has been that *at least* alternate days is best, allowing one day for presentation of poem, discussion, and — usually — writing; and the next for review, hearing from some of the children who did not get a chance to read the day before, revisions, free writing. Alternating days also gives you the latitude to accommodate completing the previous day's theme, as described above.

Monday-Wednesday-Friday is one good plan. Tuesday-Thursday also works well, later on, when a degree of interest has been established, and you might want to assign work over a period of several days.

I do not recommend five days a week of intense lessons, one following right after the next. There *is* such a thing as too much poetry.

6. **"Extras"**: Here are some things you can do to encourage further involvement with poetry:

Publication: A class literary magazine can be done inexpensively (ditto masters) and with the participation of everyone. The process of selecting each child's best or favorite poem for inclusion develops in them a necessary critical sense of their own work. Publication is, after all, the hoped-for ideal of the professional writer. Do *not* hold out the possibility of publication as a singleminded goal to work for. Wait until the lessons are coming to an end before you bring up this idea, or it will overwhelm the writing itself.

Poetry show-and-tell: Set aside a few days for independent research, during which the children are asked to go to the library, or to look through their books at home, and come up with a poem they particularly like. Ask them to bring these poems in and share with the class. You can develop a whole new curriculum based upon poetry selected by children.

Poetry readings: Make an arrangement with another class, or a group of classes, for your children to read their work? Some delightful times can be had, as your class presents the fruits of its labor to others in the school. Perhaps parents could be invited. It's an appropriate way to end the year, and to reveal what's been done. The class anthologies can be handed out at the same time.

More Writing Ideas

1. **Writing to music:** This is tricky. Do not use music that is too contemporary or music with lyrics. Ask the children to concentrate and let their minds wander at the same time. Jot down thoughts as they come, to be revised later on. Try to translate the sounds into images. Where does the music take you?

It's a useful, image-encouraging exercise, which usually works better *after* the children have had some writing experience and have learned something about structure.

2. **Filling the gap:** This works well when there's a vacation or a long weekend coming up, and you don't want to lose the momentum of writing every day. As we have seen, poetry has so much to do with cumulative, documentary accounts of our experience. We ask the children to focus on this approach over a period of days, i.e.,

"We won't be back until next Wednesday. That's five days from now. Starting tonight, I'd like you to sit down, and in no more than five lines, characterize the day. Write a few lines that capture either the most significant occasion of the day for you; or that describe your mood at the time you are writing; or that discuss a person you met, a conversation you had, any detail that captures the day. Leave the next line blank, then start the next day's account. Do this every night until we get back together."

The results are fascinating, far transcending "What I Did on My Vacation."

3. "Private papers": I am indebted to John Holt for this notion. We've concentrated entirely on the process of writing in class as one that is open and designed to be shared. There must also be a place for writing, which is never seen by anyone else, and the children should understand the validity and importance of this kind of writing, too. There should be no stigma attached to the reluctance to reveal everything to everyone. This is a writing idea that should be integrated into every "new curriculum."

4. Solitude: Accompanying the previous idea, let's remember to encourage fantasy and invention *outside* the classroom as well. Remind the children that at times when they are alone, they can think of good ideas for poems: to simply lie in bed in their own rooms at home, close their eyes, and let their minds go free. It's not surprising that the directed possibility of doing this has not occurred to many children in a formal way. The more you can point out times and places in their lives when this kind of creative thought is possible, the better for their poems. We want them to bring the *background* (the substance of everyday life) into the *foreground* (poems).

A final word: When I write a poem, I am writing down things that are important to me: not objectively or abstractly significant, not ideas or concepts that are *supposed* to be important — just things that strike me in a particularly different way.

I have to be receptive and open to the world, and to other people. I have to notice things happening, and recognize the importance of that very process of noticing.

As teachers in the classroom attempting to develop a sense of poetry in our students, we're trying to cultivate that act of noticing.

But suppose a child says, "I can't think of anything to write about!" Suppose, despite all your enticements, ideas, and suggestions, the child seems preoccupied with some obstructing problem? Suppose, in other words, he or she is experiencing "writer's block"?

We've got to make certain that, at some point along the line, the children understand that *all* writers — young, old, famous, undiscovered — go through periods when they are simply incapable of writing. It's natural, it's common, and it's nothing to be ashamed of.

What does *success* mean when poetry comes into the classroom? It's when we're all happy to *try*, to make the attempt!

About the author

Neil Baldwin was born in New York City in 1947. He attended Horace Mann School, the University of Rochester, the University of Manchester, England, and SUNY/Buffalo, where he received his Ph.D. in Modern American Poetry in 1973.

For several years, he taught in the New York State Poets-in-the-Schools program. He also conducted writing workshops at senior centers, libraries, community centers, colleges, rehabilitation and mental health centers, through grants from the New York State Council on the Arts, and Poets & Writers, Inc. He is currently Associate Director of Teachers & Writers Collaborative, a nonprofit arts-in-education organization.

Neil Baldwin is the author of two volumes of poetry, both published by the Salt-works Press in Martha's Vineyard, Massachusetts: *Seasons* (1976) and *On the Trial of Messages* (1978); and a descriptive catalogue of William Carlos Williams's manuscripts and letters (G.K. Hall & Co., 1978). He is editor of *The Niagara Magazine,* a journal of American, Canadian, and English poetry.

His poetry, translations, reviews, essays, and criticism have appeared in more than 60 magazines in the United States, Canada, Great Britain, and France, including: *American Poetry Review, Modern Poetry in Translation, West Coast Poetry Review, Contact, American Literature, The English Record,* and *Redbook.*

He lives in Brooklyn Heights, New York, with his wife and two children.

NOTES